OF THINGS AND STORIES

SELECTED PAPERS
ON ANCIENT ART AND ARCHITECTURE

SERIES EDITOR
MEGAN CIFARELLI

NUMBER 8
Of Things and Stories:
Current Approaches to Object Biography, Medium, and Materiality

OF THINGS AND STORIES

CURRENT APPROACHES TO OBJECT BIOGRAPHY, MEDIUM, AND MATERIALITY

edited by

Christina Marini and Lita Tzortzopoulou-Gregory

Archaeological Institute of America
Boston, MA
2024

OF THINGS AND STORIES

ISBN 978-1-931909-46-4

Cover design by Susanne Wilhelm. Front cover: Pitcher from the Berthouville treasure (detail); scenes from the Trojan War; first century C.E. (Paris, Bibliothèque nationale de France, Département des Monnaies, Médailles et Antiques, inv. 56.5; source gallica. bnf.fr / Bibliothèque nationale de France). Back cover: Teapot from a Greek café in Australia; 20th century C.E. (courtesy of T. and S. Poulos; photograph by P. Diacopoulos)

Library of Congress Cataloging-in-Publication Data: 2023051746

Printed in the United States on acid-free paper.

Contents

Series Editor's Preface

In 2012, The Samuel H. Kress Foundation committed to a generous, ongoing contribution to the Archaeological Institute of America's mission of promoting archaeological research and disseminating it to a broad audience in a timely fashion, through the creation of the series Selected Papers in Ancient Art and Architecture (SPAAA). The SPAAA series showcases innovative and methodologically sophisticated scholarship on art-historical topics presented at the Archaeological Institute of America Annual Meetings, with the goal of having the printed volume available for purchase at the following Annual Meeting and online through ISD (https://www.isdistribution.com/).

While this grant was initially conceived of as a highlights of art-historical research at the Archaeological Institute of America (AIA) meetings, it soon became apparent that the open sessions and organized colloquia provided excellent opportunities for creating coherent, useful volumes, often supplemented with standout individual papers from a range of sessions. In addition to review by the editorial board, all contributions are subject to a blind peer review process and judged on their individual merit. With interruptions due to the COVID-19 pandemic, this project has yielded eight volumes of the SPAAA on a wide range of topics representing the full spectrum of art historical research presented at the AIA Annual Meetings.

Megan Cifarelli

Previous volumes in the series:
SPAAA volume 1
Beyond Iconography: Materials, Methods, and Meaning in Ancient Surface Decoration, edited by Sarah Lepinski and Susanna McFadden

SPAAA volume 2
The Consumer's Choice: Uses of Greek Figure-Decorated Pottery, edited by Thomas H. Carpenter, Elizabeth Langridge Noti, and Mark D. Stansbury O'Donnell

SPAAA volume 3
What Shall I Say of Clothes? Theoretical and Methodological Approaches to the Study of Dress in Antiquity, edited by Megan Cifarelli and Laura Gawlinski

SPAAA volume 4
Collecting and Collectors: From Antiquity to Modernity, edited by Alexandra Carpino, Tiziana D'Angelo, Maya Muratov, and David Saunders

SPAAA volume 5
Emperors in Images, Architecture, and Ritual. Augustus to Fausta, edited by Francesco de Angelis

SPAAA volume 6
Roman Sculpture in Context, edited by Peter D. De Staebler and Anne Hrychuk Kontokosta

SPAAA Volume 7
Hephaistus on the Athenian Acropolis: Current Approaches to the Study of Artifacts Made of Bronze and Other Metals, edited by Nassos Papalexandrou and Amy Sowder Koch

EDITORS' PREFACE

This volume publishes a total of seven essays presented in three separate AIA-organized colloquium sessions in the 2023 Annual Meeting of the Archaeological Institute of America (New Orleans, 5–8 January 2023). All but one of the papers in the session *Of Things and Stories: The Present and Future of Object Biographies* are included, as well as four papers originally presented in the sessions titled *A Happy Medium: Media and Materiality in Ancient Art* and *Iconography and the Circulation of Roman Images,* whose organizers we thank warmly. All seven papers were selected as representative examples of different methodologies in integrating object biography, medium, and materiality.

We wish to express our thanks to all contributors for their collaboration and to the members of the Selected Papers in Ancient Art and Architecture editorial committee for presenting us with the opportunity of this publication. Our warmest thanks go to the series editor, Megan Cifarelli, for her support, guidance, and commitment throughout the process. We also thank Jon Frey for his instrumental support in organizing the session *Of Things and Stories: The Present and Future of Object Biographies* as the Medieval and Post Medieval Archaeology (MAPMA) session for the conference. Neville McFerrin attended the session and it was through her recommendation to devote this SPAAA volume on the subject of object biography and materiality that this became reality. We are immensely grateful to her for her encouragement. Last but not least, we deeply appreciate the many anonymous reviewers and editorial board readers, for their constructive suggestions and feedback.

We present this volume with the hope that it will inspire further discussion and will offer a fresh insight into materiality and the intricate interactions between things and people across space and time.

Introduction

Christina Marini and Lita Tzortzopoulou-Gregory

Materiality has been one of the core themes driving archaeological theory over the past decades. This is not by any means surprising, considering that material remains constitute one of the most abundant and readily available sources of information archaeological research can work with, but the material turn in social sciences, in combination with posthumanist thinking, have profoundly redefined how the discourse around them is structured and theoretically conceptualized. New ontological and materialist perspectives have set the discussion on new grounds, moving away from material cultures, typological variability, and interpretation, and prioritizing the multilayered and ever-changing interactions between humans and things, with varying focus on matters of agency, dependency, movement, and relationality.[1] From network, to entanglement, meshwork, correspondence, and assemblage, different concepts have functioned as distinct theoretical vehicles for tracking and analyzing these interactions, addressing in distinct—but in many ways converging—manners the parameters and facets of these relationships.[2]

This collection of essays, bringing together papers presented in the 2023 American Institute of Archaeology/Society for Classical Studies Annual Meeting in New Orleans, Louisiana, from 5–8 January 2023, endeavors to offer current material-based approaches to the highly theorized theme of materiality through the exploration of two perspectives: object biography and materiality in relation to medium. The authors utilize analytical and methodological tools informed by the advances in the theoretical discourse to present case studies spanning a wide chronological horizon, from prehistory to the present. The two topics work in dialogue with each other and their scopes function in a complementary way, looking from different angles into the ontology of things, and the complexities of the relational connections that dynamically link things and people.

Object biography is a well-established and long-lived—to use appropriately biographical phrasing—analytical construct. Its introduction by the works of A. Appadurai and I. Kopytoff was a revolutionary step in how objects and materiality in general were conceptualized and problematized.[3] It demonstrated that objects are not inert, but instead have unbounded meanings and values that are situationally defined, depending on the social, economic, and cultural frames of reference. Despite the valid criticisms about the anthropocentricism and the ontological inadequacies of the biographical metaphor, the object biographical approach remains relevant, not least because of its capacity to offer nuanced, bottom-up insights into the patterns of human–thing dependence and dependency. The current concept of the object itinerary, in fact, showcases how the approach has been refined, updated, and adapted to accommodate the theoretical advances and paradigm shifts in the discourse on materiality. Developed from two different but relevant starting points, object itinerary successfully attempts to amend misleading impressions stemming from the biographical metaphor, and more specifically the linearity of the biographical construct, which created the misconception that things have finite lives, with clearly definable beginnings and endings.[4] More importantly, by placing emphasis on the notion of nonlinear mobility, object itinerary encompasses the concept of movement—physical, as well as metaphorical, through time and space—that has been central in materiality theorizations of the past decades.[5]

Amidst the rapid evolution of theoretical approaches, object biography and itinerary, as its ontological successor, have not outlived their methodological value and retain their analytical usefulness first and foremost because they remain an indispensable tool for exploring individual material artifacts in a holistic way. They offer the opportunity to investigate the complexities of human-object entanglement, or the meshworks of their interactions on an individualized scale, with the potential to construct narratives that shed light into broader social and cultural phenomena. Examining how the things themselves are in an ever-progressing state of becoming, deeply and concurrently connected with the lives and realities of different humans, as well as the itineraries of other things, biographical approaches demonstrate how humans and things can only be understood in conjunction with each other. At the same time, the familiarity of the metaphor and the inherent narrative structure of both biography and itinerary create a compelling framework that alleviates—without obliterating—the theoretically charged load that objects have come to carry in the discourse.

The exploration of issues associated with medium, on the other hand focuses more closely on the processes of becoming and the interplay between substance and the meanings, significance, and values ascribed to things. Medium emerges as an element that is beyond strictly matter. It is perceived as being in motion, instead of being static, or characterized by rigidly fixed attributes.[6] Material properties within the current theoretical debate are understood as relational and dynamic. As such, medium functions as an interface between the physical, tangible aspects of objects and the nonrepresentational relations they are part of in the material, socioeconomic, cultural, and other contexts they are embedded in. From this standpoint, form and substance are means of negotiating, mediating, and communicating meaning, and can be equally imbued with agency. They are thus perceived as malleable, displaying qualities that reflect situationally defined states of power or value.

The above outlined theoretical concepts, whose brief summary cannot possibly do justice to the diversity and depth of current approaches surrounding materialisms and materiality in social sciences in general and archaeology in specific, provided the foundations upon which this volume is grounded and determined the selection of essays presented here. The seven papers that comprise the current installment of *Selected Papers in Ancient Art and Architecture* were originally presented in three sessions of 2023 American Institute of Archaeology/Society for Classical Studies Annual Meeting, titled: *Of Things and Stories: The Present and Future of Object Biographies* (Hammond; Canós-Donnay and de Groot; Marini and Tzortzopoulou-Gregory), *A Happy Medium: Media and Materiality in Ancient Art* (Phillips; Rumora; Vander Horst), and *Iconography and the Circulation of Roman Images* (Petrain). The papers examine distinct case studies that function as representative examples of different methodologies integrating theoretical advances on object biography/itinerary, and materiality in relation to medium. Their focus spreads across a wide temporal and spatial horizon, within and beyond the ancient Mediterranean, contributing to interdisciplinary discussions on the study of things. Mirroring the title and theme of the volume, the contributions are organized in two groups, with the first four chapters discussing object biographical topics and the last three handling subjects on medium; within these two groups the chapters are presented chronologically, according to the date range of the objects and subject matter.

Starting with Mark Hammond's chapter, the biography of one humble object from a funerary assemblage of Late Roman date excavated in 1933 in Corinth is used to highlight the conscious actions taken by the different human players who came to interact with it. Through the lens of object biography, by tracing the life cycle of this seemingly unremarkable lekythos from production to distribution, short-lived use, discard and centuries-long burial, and rediscovery by its excavator, Hammond explores its connection to larger cultural and economic systems as well as the ritual practices of Late Roman Corinth and its surrounding region.

From a modest, mass-produced Late Roman lekythos serving a ritual function in a mortuary context, the subject of the next chapter of this volume focuses on the itinerary of two Roman luxury items that ended up in the possession of a Romanized Celt in Gaul. By combining an object itinerary approach with iconographic analysis, David Petrain traces the journey of the two silver pitchers belonging to the Berthouville treasure, from Italy to a sanctuary on the periphery of the Roman Empire. A reinterpretation of the Trojan War depictions on the pitchers, drawing attention to the recurring image of Achilles's shield and its own life cycle, is used by the author to argue for an analogous journey of the pitchers themselves, connecting everyone who interacted with the objects through their own biographies.

An object itinerary approach is also followed by the next two chapters. Sirio Canós-Donnay and Beatrijs de Groot present the long and complex trajectories that entangled a jar kept in a convent in Salamanca, Spain, and Teresa Chikaba, an 18th-century Afro-Hispanic nun, slave, and writer. The journey of this jar of Ottoman origin, claimed to be made of clay with healing properties from the Greek island of Lemnos, to its current location within a convent display case is presented by the authors as part of a multilayered web of entangled cross-cultural histories shaped by material processes, economy, politics, and religion.

The chapter by Christina Marini and Lita Tzortzopoulou-Gregory uses object itinerary to explore the intersection of the materiality of migration and modern diasporas by focusing on the journeys of three teapots belonging to three different individuals. The objects and people examined are connected through the transnational experience of Greek-Australian migrants from the island of Kythera and the iconic establishments of Greek cafés in Australia. The study follows the itineraries of the three vessels from the manufacturing process, to their circulation and use in Australia during the 20th century, and their present-day symbolically charged status in domestic assemblages on Kythera.

Turning to issues of materiality and medium, Rachel Phillips's study takes a look into elite mortuary practices in the Bronze Age Aegean. Using Shaft Graves IV and V from Grave Circle A at Mycenae as a starting point, the author offers a reassessment of the use of gold foil in Mycenaean burial customs, and explores the processes through which the body of the deceased was transformed from subject to object with the affective use of gold. The interplay of the material qualities of gold and the symbolic language of the ritual emerges as a field for constructing a distinct image of the deceased, merging the buried individual with the material funerary assemblage.

A new approach to Roman freestanding statuary is followed by Roko Rumora, who focuses on the medium-specific qualities of sculptures in architectural settings, and their entanglement with the relationships that developed around urban euergetism. Using the aedicular façades of the theater and the library of Celsus in Ephesus as case studies, he argues that Roman patrons were acutely aware of the materiality of the statues and the potential of statuary to mediate values and ideas when combined with other visual means, such as architecture or inscriptions, with the aim to meet or challenge their audience's expectations.

Moving geographically westward to Britain, the final chapter of the volume introduces a different approach to understanding Romano-British face pots as active agents in votive and funerary contexts. Building on anthropological perspectives, Danielle Vander Horst puts forward the idea that pre-Roman conceptions of the human body in Iron Age Britain had an effect on the perception and uses of the face pots in Britain as opposed to the continent. Through an examination of distribution patterns and variability of formal characteristics in combination with notions of materiality and embodiment, the author investigates how local and pre-Roman beliefs impacted material behaviors and consumption patterns in relation to a distinctive class of objects in the Roman world.

The array of essays presented here demonstrates the varied, although certainly not exhaustive, approaches to examining the ever-transforming meanings of objects and their complex relationships with the humans they interact with, which are neither linear nor unidirectional. Each study offers a unique case of storytelling where objects are intertwined with people, within different systems of beliefs and values, and become entangled with broader cross-cultural, socioeconomic, and political spheres.

Notes

[1] For works that set the tone for the discourse, see, e.g., Gosden 2005; Tilley 2007; Knappett and Malafouris 2008; Hicks 2010; Hodder 2012; Harris and Cipolla 2017; Harrison-Buck and Hendon 2018. For symmetrical approaches, see Olsen 2003, 2010; Shanks 2007; Witmore 2007; Webmoor and Witmore 2008; Olsen and Witmore 2015. For posthumanist perspectives, see Sørensen 2013; Harris and Crellin 2018; Crellin and Harris 2021.

[2] Network: Latour 2005; Knappett and Malafouris 2008; Knappett 2011, 2013. Entanglement: Hodder 2011, 2012, 2014. Meshwork: Ingold 2007a, 2011. Correspondence: Ingold 2015, 2017. Assemblage: Fowler 2013; Harris 2014; Lucas 2017; Jervis 2018. See also Antczak and Beaudry (2019) for assemblage of practice, an analytical tool attempting to bring together the variety of theoretical concepts in one methodological framework.

[3] Appadurai 1986; Kopytoff 1986. For archaeological applications, see, e.g., Hoskins 1998; Gosden and Marshall 1999 and all papers in the same installment of *World Archaeology*; Fontijn 2002; Holtorf 2002; Meskell 2004; Joy 2009.

[4] Hahn and Weiss 2013; Joyce and Gillespie 2015.

[5] Bauer 2019, 343–44.

[6] Ingold 2007b.

Works Cited

Antczak, K.A., and M.C. Beaudry. 2019. "Assemblages of Practice: A Conceptual Framework for Exploring Human–Thing Relations in Archaeology." *Archaeological Dialogues* 26:87–110. DOI: 10.1017/S1380203819000205.

Appadurai, A. 1986. "Introduction: Commodities and the Politics of Value." In *The Social Life of Things: Commodities in*

Cultural Perspective, edited by A. Appadurai, 3–63. Cambridge: Cambridge University Press. DOI: 10.1017/CBO9780511819582.003.

Bauer, A.A. 2019. "Itinerant Objects." *Annual Review of Anthropology* 48:335–52. DOI: 10.1146/annurev-anthro-102218-011111.

Crellin, R.J., and O.J.T. Harris. 2021. "What Difference Does Posthumanism Make?" *CAJ* 31:469–75. DOI: 10.1017/S0959774321000159.

Fontijn, D.R. 2002. *Sacrificial Landscapes: Cultural Biographies of Persons, Objects and "Natural" Places in the Bronze Age of the Southern Netherlands, c. 2300–600BC*. Leiden: University of Leiden.

Fowler, C. 2013. "Dynamic Assemblages, or the Past Is What Endures: Change and the Duration of Relations." In *Archaeology after Interpretation, Returning Materials to Archaeological Theory*, edited by B. Alberti, A.M. Jones, and J. Pollard, 235–56. Walnut Creek, CA: Left Coast Press.

Gosden, C. 2005. "What Do Objects Want?" *Journal of Archaeological Method and Theory* 12:193–211. DOI: 10.1007/s10816-005-6928-x.

Gosden, C., and Y. Marshall. 1999. "The Cultural Biography of Objects." *WorldArch* 31:169–78. DOI: 10.1080/00438243.1999.9980439.

Hahn, H.P., and H. Weiss, eds. 2013. *Mobility, Meaning and the Transformations of Things: Shifting Contexts of Material Culture through Time and Space*. Oxford: Oxbow.

Harris, O.J.T. 2014. "(Re)assembling Communities." *Journal of Archaeological Method and Theory* 21:76–97. DOI: 10.1007/s10816-012-9138-3.

Harris, O.J.T., and C.N. Cipolla. 2017. *Archaeological Theory in the New Millennium: Introducing Current Perspectives*. Abingdon and New York: Routledge.

Harris, O.J.T., and R.J. Crellin. 2018. "Assembling New Ontologies from Old Materials: Towards Multiplicity." In *Rethinking Relations and Animism: Personhood and Materiality*, edited by M. Astor-Aguilera and G. Harvey, 55–74. Abingdon: Routledge.

Harrison-Buck, E., and J.A. Hendon, eds. 2018. *Relational Identities and Other-Than-Human Agency in Archaeology*. Boulder: University Press of Colorado.

Hicks, D. 2010. "The Material–Cultural Turn: Event and Effect." In *The Oxford Handbook of Material Culture Studies*, edited by D. Hicks and M.C. Beaudry, 24–98. Oxford: Oxford University Press. DOI: 10.1093/oxfordhb/9780199218714.013.0002.

Hodder, I. 2011. "Human-Thing Entanglement: Towards an Integrated Archaeological Perspective." *JRAI* 17:154–77. DOI:

10.1111/j.1467-9655.2010.01674.x.

———. 2012. *Entangled: An Archaeology of the Relationships between Humans and Things*. Malden: Wiley-Blackwell.

———. 2014. "The Entanglements of Humans and Things: A Long-Term View." *New Literary History* 45:19–36.

Holtorf, C.J. 2002. "Notes on the Life History of a Pot Sherd." *Journal of Material Culture* 7:49–71. DOI: 10.1177/1359183502007001.

Hoskins, J. 1998. *Biographical Objects: How Things Tell the Stories of People's Lives*. London: Routledge.

Ingold, T. 2007a. *Lines: A Brief History*. London: Routledge.

———. 2007b. "Materials against Materiality." *Archaeological Dialogues* 14:1–16. DOI: 10.1017/S1380203807002127.

———. 2011. *Being Alive: Essays on Movement, Knowledge and Description*. London: Routledge.

———. 2015. *The Life of Lines*. London: Routledge.

———. 2017. "On Human Correspondence." *JRAI* 23:9–27. DOI: 10.1111/1467-9655.12541.

Jervis, B. 2018. *Assemblage Thought and Archaeology*. Abingdon: Routledge.

Joy, J. 2009. "Reinvigorating Object Biography: Reproducing the Drama of Object Lives." *WorldArch* 4:540–56. DOI: 10.1080/00438240903345530.

Joyce, R.A., and S.D. Gillespie, eds. 2015. *Things in Motion: Object Itineraries in Anthropological Practice*. Santa Fe: SAR Press.

Knappett, C. 2011. *An Archaeology of Interaction: Network Perspectives on Material Culture and Society*. Oxford: Oxford University Press.

———, ed. 2013. *Network Analysis in Archaeology: New Approaches to Regional Interaction*. Oxford: Oxford University Press.

Knappett, C, and L. Malafouris, eds. 2008. *Material Agency: Towards a Non-Anthropocentric Approach*. New York: Springer.

Kopytoff, I. 1986. "The Cultural Biography of Things: Commoditization as Process." In *The Social Life of Things: Commodities in Cultural Perspective*, edited by A. Appadurai, 64–91. Cambridge: Cambridge University Press. DOI: 10.1017/CBO9780511819582.004.

Latour, B. 2005. *Reassembling the Social: An Introduction to Actor-Network-Theory*. Oxford: Oxford University Press.

Lucas, G. 2017. "Variations on a Theme: Assemblage Archaeology." *CAJ* 7:187–90. DOI: 10.1017/S0959774316000573.

Meskell, L. 2004. *Object Worlds in Ancient Egypt: Material Biographies Past and Present*. Oxford: Berg.

Olsen, B. 2003. "Material Culture after Text: Re-Membering Things." *Norwegian Archaeological Review* 36:87–104. DOI: 10.1080/00293650310000650.

———. 2010. *In Defense of Things: Archaeology and the Ontology of Objects*. Lanham, MD: Altamira.

Olsen, B., and C. Witmore. 2015. "Archaeology, Symmetry and the Ontology of Things: A Response to Critics." *Archaeological Dialogues* 22:187–97. DOI: 10.1017/ S1380203815000240.

Shanks, M. 2007. "Symmetrical Archaeology." *WorldArch* 39:589–96. DOI: 10.1080/00438240701679676.

Sørensen, T.F. 2013: "We Have Never Been Latourian. Archaeological Ethics and the Posthuman Condition." *Norwegian Archaeological Review* 46:1–18. DOI: 10.1080/00293652.2013.779317.

Tilley, C. 2007. "Materiality in Materials." *Archaeological Dialogues* 14:16–20. DOI: 10.1017/S1380203807002139.

Webmoor, T., and C. Witmore. 2008. "Things Are Us! A Commentary on Human/Things Relations under the Banner of a 'Social' Archaeology." *Norwegian Archaeological Review* 41:53–70. DOI: 10.1080/00293650701698423.

Witmore, C. 2007. "Symmetrical Archaeology: Excerpts of a Manifesto." *WorldArch* 39:546–62. DOI: 10.1080/00438240701679411.

Memoirs of a Late Roman Lekythos: Insights from the Hill of Zeus, Corinth

Mark D. Hammond

Abstract

In 1933 the American School of Classical Studies in Athens (ASCSA) dug four trial trenches on the so-called Hill of Zeus in ancient Corinth, Greece, revealing several Late Roman graves (late-sixth to early seventh century C.E.) with associated pottery. Analysis of just one of the ceramic vessels, a coarse, undecorated lekythos, through the lens of object biography can illuminate the meanings attached to the object by the potters, distributors, market-goers, bereaved, and even the modern excavator during their interactions with it at different stages of its life cycle. Insights drawn from archaeological ceramic analysis, ancient and modern Greek funerary practice, and experience in the modern ceramic studio are all marshaled to provide deeper understanding of each stage of meaning. By mapping the biography of just one vessel from this assemblage it is possible to comment on the craft traditions, the economy, and the ritual practices of Corinth and its surrounding region in the Late Roman period.[1]

Introduction

THIS STUDY FOCUSES ON A RATHER UNDERSTUDIED VESSEL shape—the ceramic, Late Roman lekythos. Unlike Late Roman fine wares, Late Roman lekythoi are more difficult to study due to their simple manufacture, lack of decoration, and regional nature. Although the basic form is widespread in Greece, chronology and typology are undefined, and their function is typically not probed deeper than noting their presence in funerary contexts.[2] However, by examining one example through the lens of object biography, it will be demonstrated that there is much that can be learned from these humble objects. Object biography acknowledges that objects, like people, have life spans during which the object may be a participant in events, changes can be made to it (whether physically or conceptually), and reciprocal transformations occur between user and object as they interact. Object biography seeks to understand how meaning becomes invested in objects through these interactions, but these meanings are not static and can be reinterpreted with each interaction.[3] As will be seen with this lekythos, meanings can be subjectively positive or negative. Moreover, although this vessel was a necessary component of a highly charged cultural and religious event, it will be demonstrated that it was never considered anything akin to a "gift," which would maintain meaningful links between the parties of the transaction. Rather, it was viewed more as a commodity by its maker and user(s) in that it was alienable, leaving no lasting relationship between giver and receiver.[4] In the context of the Late Roman funeral it was part of, it was a commodity to be used and disposed of. This alienation was continued by its excavator, who ignored its study completely. This study will describe every major stage of this object's use-life, from its creation to excavation, while incorporating a biographical approach that will illustrate how the unique interactions with the object in the past inform researchers today about craft traditions, the economy, and the ritual practices of Late Roman Corinth and its surrounding region.

The object in question is a simple Late Roman lekythos, numbered C-1933-1524 (figs. 1, 2).[5] Lekythoi are small, one-handled vessels, characterized by their narrow mouths making them suitable for the slow pouring of oil or wine. Although subject to a variety of uses, these forms are often found in pre-Christian and Christian funerary contexts where they were used to make graveside liquid offerings. The lekythos C-1933-1524 is complete, minus a chip from the rim, with a height of 14.1 cm.[6] Its near-vertical walls taper into a thin neck with a tall concave rim, and are decorated with two roughly incised lines at the shoulder. A simple handle is attached at the shoulder and the lower rim. Through macroscopic analysis, the fabric has been identified as a refined version of southern Argolid fabric (discussed below).[7] While this object lacks a precise date, comparanda from Corinth and Athens suggest a date of the late sixth or seventh century.[8] In what follows, the lekythos's lifespan is charted backward through time, beginning with its modern excavation and ending with its manufacture.

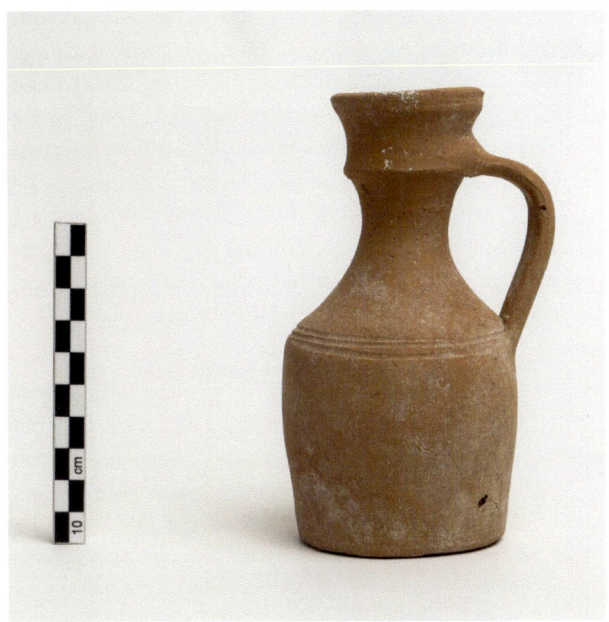

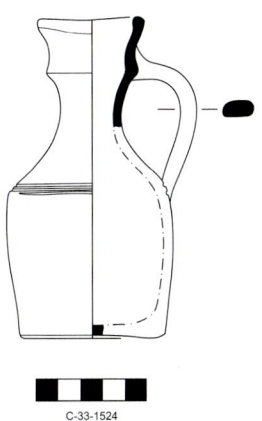

Fig. 1 (left). Photograph of lekythos C-1933-1524 (photograph by P. Dellatolas; American School of Classical Studies at Athens, Corinth Excavations; by permission of the Hellenic Ministry of Culture and Sports, Archaeological Resources Fund).

Fig. 2 (above). Profile of lekythos C-1933-1524 (drawing by C. Kolb; American School of Classical Studies at Athens, Corinth Excavations; by permission of the Hellenic Ministry of Culture and Sports, Archaeological Resources Fund).

Excavation and Initial Treatment

The excavations of the so-called Hill of Zeus, situated along Corinth's northern ridge, were conducted in 1933 under the auspices of the American School of Classical Studies in Athens. Lekythos C-1933-1524 was recovered from Grave 33 (also G273, but now Grave 1933-162 in the current record keeping system) within trial trench 1. F.J. de Waele directed the excavations after uncovering Corinth's Asklepieion and Lerna Court, intending to explore the western hill overlooking the site to test Pausanias's (2.4.5) account that a temple to Zeus stood nearby (fig. 3). Certainly, de Waele would have felt a good deal of disappointment after his team spent 18 days in the four trial trenches digging down to bedrock, uncovering no trace of a temple, but instead revealing numerous Late Roman Christian graves.[9]

The results of the excavations were recorded in Corinth Notebook 138, and include the only plan of the graves before they were reburied. Although each grave was labeled, additional architectural features that are depicted are not discussed at all. The notebook is characterized by its paucity of notes followed by numerous blank pages, almost as if the excavator had simply lost interest. A single line in a 1935 report is the only published mention of this excavation by de Waele himself, and the final publication of the Asklepieion and Lerna says little more.[10]

While de Waele was silent about his disappointing finds, his predecessors were more vocal in their criticisms. To the west of the Hill of Zeus, trench II was dug in 1896 during the first year of ASCSA excavations at Corinth, uncovering 14 similarly described (see below) rock-cut graves (13 opened), whose contents (not saved, or now missing) can be assumed to be analogous to those from the Hill of Zeus. The report of this inaugural campaign described the graves as follows:

> About half of these contained pottery; but it was all coarse, unglazed, unpointed [*sic*] red ware, which could lay no claim to great antiquity. It is possible that these graves are more ancient than their contents, and were old Corinthian graves rifled by the Roman settlers ... and then put to a secondary use by the generation which plundered them. We opened in all thirteen graves. One was cut entirely below the level of the others, and ran partly under two of them, so that here our hope was especially keen that this might have escaped plunder and might yield something of value; but its contents differed in no respect from those of the others.[11]

Surely, de Waele had similar opinions in 1933, but recognized enough value in these objects to at least place them into storage. Nevertheless, the ceramic objects recovered from the Hill of Zeus, including C-1933-1524, were, for the most part, ignored.[12]

The Funerary Context

The graves of the Hill of Zeus were part of a larger cemetery landscape that is today referred to as the Cemetery of Lerna Hollow, a mostly late-sixth to seventh-century cemetery that incorporates the Late Roman graves from the 1896 trial trench, the Asklepieion, Lerna Court, the Hill of Zeus, and Wiseman's excavations of the gymnasium area (fig. 3). Lekythos C-1933-1524 was recovered in Grave 33, classified by de Waele as his "rock-cut grave, type 1" (fig. 4), a type that commonly appears throughout the cemetery.[13] Type 1 graves were made by first excavating a square, vertical shaft less than one meter square down into over one meter of soft bedrock,

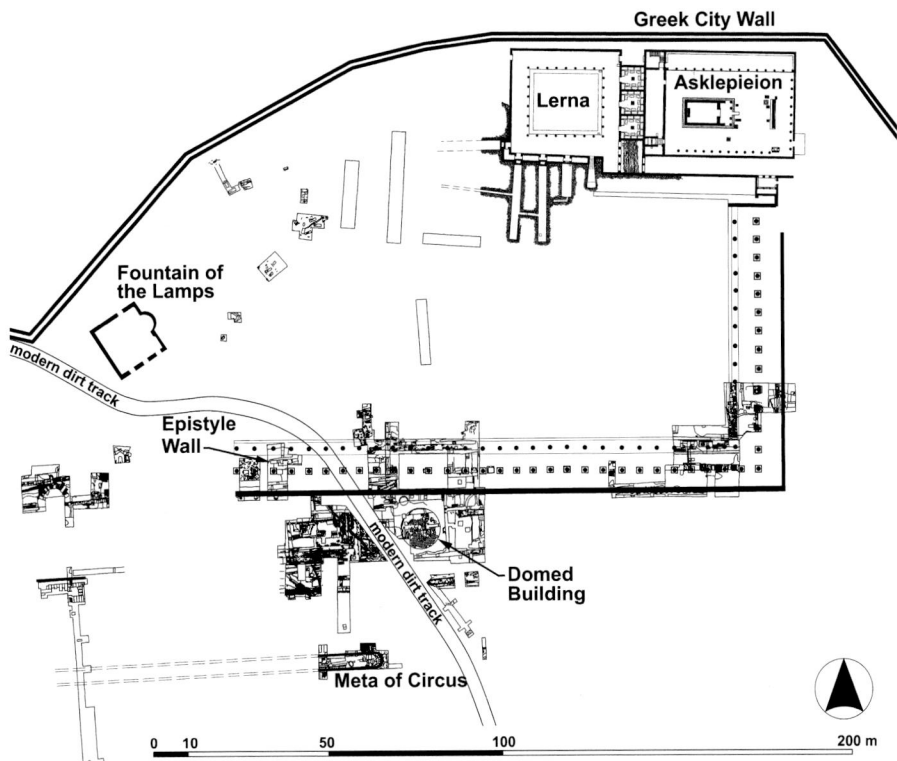

Fig. 3. Plan of the Cemetery of Lerna Hollow area. The four Hill of Zeus trenches are indicated near the middle of the plan, just southwest of Lerna (drawing by J. Herbst; American School of Classical Studies at Athens, Corinth Excavations; by permission of the Hellenic Ministry of Culture and Sports, Archaeological Resources Fund).

then a horizontal chamber about two meters long toward the west. The vertical shaft was sealed with a square, stone slab. Later excavations from the gymnasium area indicate that the body would have been placed head-first into the L-shaped tomb, with the feet in the shaft. A mound of earth and stone was built on top and covered in stucco, sometimes incorporating the funerary pottery into the matrix of its construction instead of placing them in the tomb.[14] Any future internments would have required the removal of part of the mound to expose the shaft, and then its subsequent reconstruction after a new body was placed inside.

From the preserved records, we know that C-1933-1524 was one of at least eight (if not 13) vessels recovered from Grave 33.[15] These included lekythoi in various fabrics, pitchers, fine ware mugs, and a bowl stamped with a cross. The human remains from the Hill of Zeus were either lost or were not kept at all, nor did de Waele generally make note of them. Grave 33 is the only grave for which details about bodies and the position of finds were made. Among the "many

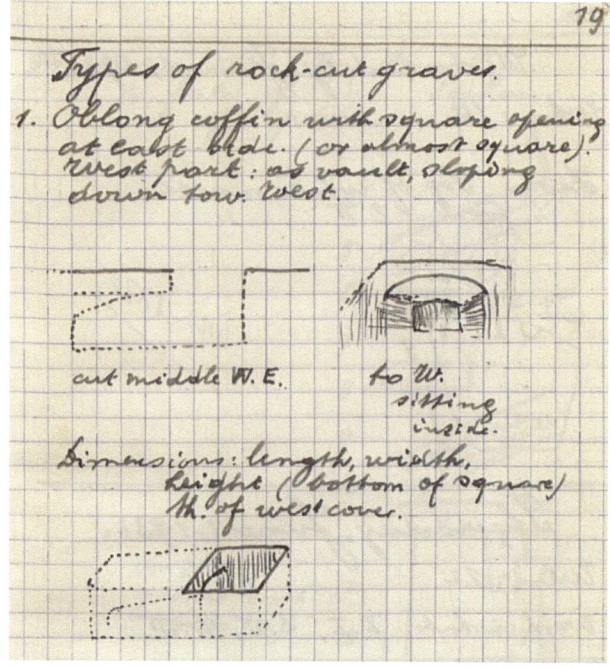

heads (+/- 8)," vessels were noted at the feet, in the middle, and at the head, inside this one-meter-wide, L-shaped shaft.[16] Lekythos C-1933-1524 was therefore included in a very crowded grave.

The question of what purpose C-1933-1524 and the other ceramics from Grave 33 served is another issue to consider. The bowl (with stamped cross), and perhaps the mugs and pitchers, could conceivably have been associated with a grave-side funerary meal, but lekythoi like C-1933-1524 seem to have served another purpose.[17] Since lekythoi are closed shapes with narrow mouths, they are appropriate for the slow pouring of liquid contents. In examining the burial customs of Late Roman Greece alongside modern Orthodox burial customs, two features seem particularly relevant: the anointing of the body with a liquid libation just before final burial, and the sense of uncleanliness or pollution to any food, drink, or vessels remaining after a funeral service is complete necessitating their disposal.[18] Some have postulated that the custom of actively breaking pottery after a funeral began sometime in the seventh century.[19] In some modern accounts, when the church bells toll to signal the procession to the graveyard, any water still standing in a vessel in the village should be thrown out, and the vessel itself broken, while other accounts record that no food from the meals at the graveyard may reenter the home.[20]

Given the awkward and small shape of these rock-cut chamber tombs (type 1), if C-1933-1524 was used for making a libation over the body, it must have happened in the open air before the body was interred. Moreover, once the lekythos was utilized in this funerary context, there would have been no desire to take this polluted vessel home. Some of the broken vessels from other graves may have been deliberately smashed, while others were built into the matrix of the overlying mounds (see above) to dispose of them. Likewise, mourners chose to dispose of C-1933-1524 within the cemetery, with the open tomb offering a convenient alternative.[21] Again, considering the awkward L-shape of Grave 33, C-1933-1524 and the accompanying vessels were likely placed near the feet within the vertical shaft and then subsequently pushed farther back along the horizontal shaft as new internments were added, with the result that their final positions may have been at the feet, middle, or head. Several vessels in Grave 33 are still intact, and many only feature a broken rim and/or handle. Rims and handles are sensitive areas for any vessel, and those that were left standing during previous burials may have been knocked over during subsequent burials. This was possibly the case for C-1933-1524, whose rim may have been chipped when it fell as the "plus/minus eight" bodies were interred.

Distribution and Purchase in the Late Roman Period

Forty-three vessels from the Hill of Zeus were entered into the excavation's catalogue. Of those, at least 26 come from regional sources.[22] Eleven vessels, including C-1933-1524, can be identified as having employed southern Argolid fabric in their manufacture.[23] The shapes of these 11 include two lekythoi each of a unique shape, one small, broken pitcher, and eight lekythoi similar in shape to C-1933-1524.[24] A coarser version of this fabric was used in the manufacture of the Late Roman Amphora 2, suggesting a shared area of production. Kilns producing these amphoras were found during a survey in modern Kounoupi, southeast of Porto Cheli on the southern tip of the Argolid peninsula.[25]

Given the multiplicity of fabrics in which lekythoi appear at Corinth, it seems unlikely that distribution from the southern Argolid to Corinth was driven by a need for funerary lekythoi, since they were readily available from multiple sources. The most likely scenario is that in which southern Argolid lekythoi were "piggybacking" on the state-sponsored distribution of products shipped in the Late Roman Amphora 2.[26] Distribution moved north along the coast before reaching Corinth's eastern harbor at Kenchreai, where the Late Roman Amphora 2 shipments could have been loaded into larger sea-going vessels. Shipments of smaller objects, like C-1933-1524, could have been loaded after the main cargo as space allowed, and sold at the next port-of-call. While consumers in Corinth were likely not eagerly awaiting the next shipment of southern Argolid lekythoi before they could bury their dead, death is a certainty in life that would have ensured that funerary vessels witnessed steady consumption, and that at least some profit could be made by this commodity. Clearly, C-1933-1524 was successfully obtained from a distributor and brought to the cemetery for its use. It will never be known whether this lekythos was obtained through purchase, trade, or charity, nor if its objective shortcomings (see below) warranted any sort of discounted value.

Not every vessel placed in a burial is necessarily representative of some meaning generated between user and object through previous interactions. Some of the vessels in Grave 33, such as the pitchers, fine ware mugs, and stamped bowl, *might* have originally been household objects reused at the grave as similar objects are also represented in nonfunerary contexts in Corinth.[27] For C-1933-1524 and other similar Late Roman lekythoi that do not regularly appear in nonfunerary contexts, however, it is far more likely that the relationship between these shapes and their users had more to do with utility and opportunity, and their deposition (or, more accurately, disposal) was guided by a sense of pollution. To examine this point further, it is useful to examine this object's life at its very earliest stage—its production.

Workshop Production

At some point near the beginning of the seventh century C.E., a potter working in the southern Argolid used the same fabric employed in the Late Roman Amphora 2, albeit in a refined state, to manufacture C-1933-1524. Southern Argolid fabric, whether in its coarse or refined state, was utilized in several different classes and shapes, including coarse basins

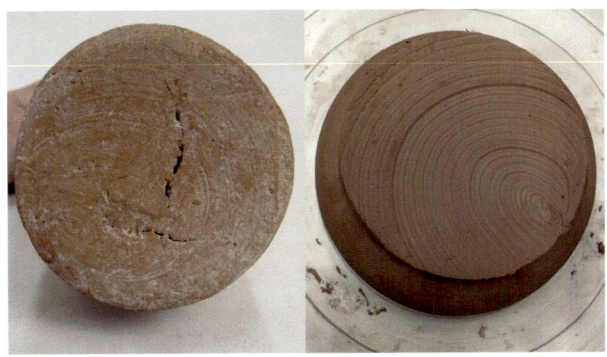

Fig. 5. Photograph of the base of C-1933-1524 (left) with comparative photograph of the base of a newly thrown vessel in a modern ceramic studio (right).

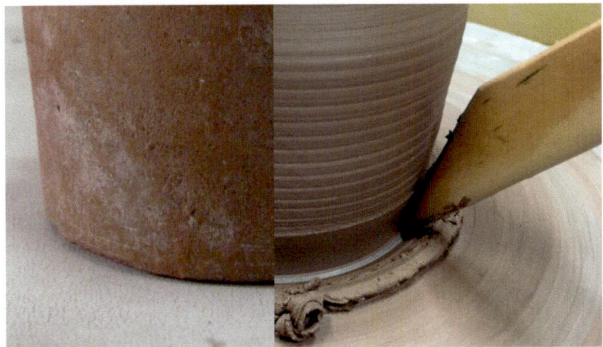

Fig. 6. Detail of the lower portion of C-1933-1524 (left) with comparative photograph illustrating the removal of slurry from the base of a newly thrown vessel in a modern ceramic studio (right).

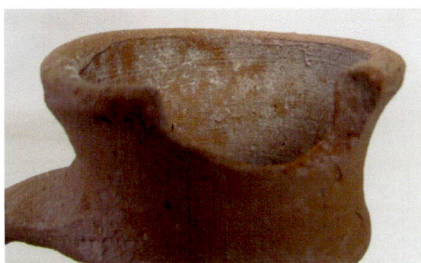

Fig. 8. Detail of the rim of C-1933-1524.

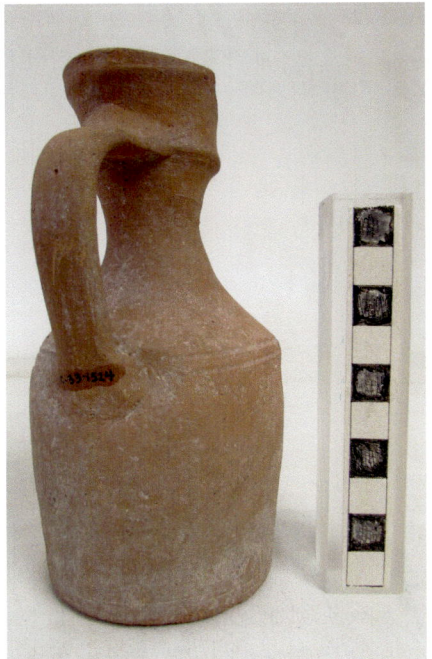

Fig. 7. Detail of the handle of C-1933-1524.

and pitchers, and thinner-walled bowls and lamps.[28] That lekythoi were manufactured utilizing the same raw materials is no surprise.

However, C-1933-1524, and other southern Argolid lekythoi, possess several objective shortcomings. R.B. Richardson's description of the finds from trench II of 1896 was more accurate and insightful than he probably thought, as these vessels are indeed "coarse, unglazed, unpainted." Furthermore, from a studio ceramics perspective, they feature more instances of shortcuts and mistakes than are typically noted in Roman ceramics. With some experience in the modern 21st-century pottery studio, one is able to note features specific to C-1933-1524 that indicate that it was formed and finished simply, quickly, and with little regard for aesthetic perfection.[29]

Beginning at the bottom, the vessel was string-cut with no articulation of the base. That is, a string was used to sever the finished vessel from the wheel after it was formed, with no additional trimming or finishing—for comparison, similar markings were achieved while string-cutting a vessel in the modern pottery studio while it was still spinning at medium speed on the electric wheel (fig. 5). The potter of C-1933-1524 did, however, take the time to remove any wet clay, or slurry, that accumulated around the base before cutting it free with the string (fig. 6). This is evidenced by the small bevel around the clean edge of the base formed after using a small tool to scrape along the bottom while the wheel is in motion. However, the cracks on the base of C-1933-1524 indicate that the vessel was not properly dried before being placed in the kiln for firing (fig. 5). The excess moisture in the base expanded when fired, implying that its manufacture was somewhat rushed. This crack, however, is not deep enough to have marred the functionality of this vessel.

Some fingerprints and streaks are visible on the body upon close inspection testifying to the handling of the vessel while still wet, but these are not overly excessive (unlike other examples from the Hill of Zeus). The handle, however, is not perfectly vertical but was aligned slightly off-axis. Moreover, because the vessel was still too wet, the pressure applied to the walls while the handle was being attached dented the surface of the vessel at the shoulder (fig. 7). The rim is not even, but appears wavy (fig. 8). This occurs when the clay is not properly centered on the wheel before the vessel begins to be formed, or if the clay is pulled unevenly during the formation process. Most obviously, there is no slip, glaze, or painted decoration. The only decoration consists of two roughly incised lines at the shoulder. These were spirally incised, achieved by pressing a tool against the wall of the vessel while still spinning on the wheel. A line belonging to a third rotation lasts for only five centimeters before the process was aborted. The technique is simple and can easily be achieved by a novice. Nevertheless, the completed lines are quite uneven.

While it is difficult to apply modern standards to premodern ceramic vessels, these features suggest that C-1933-1524 and similar vessels were objects of rapid mass-production. The hurried manner of production may even suggest that their one-time use at the graveside was anticipated by the potters themselves. This lekythos was created by a potter who knew that its interactions with its future user(s) would not generate any significant meaning beyond its immediate functional use, that it would become polluted, and would require immediate disposal.

Conclusion

Lekythos C-1933-1524 was never a gift to the dead, but was more a commodity, an alienable object not intended to generate meaning beyond its moment of purpose. It was created by a potter who anticipated its disposable nature, distributed with the knowledge that it would not fulfill a desperate commercial need, used by mourners who attached a sense of pollution to it, and excavated by an archaeologist who disdained it for not reflecting an era better attested in classical literature. Despite this lekythos's valuation as a disposable commodity during its lifetime, the social actions it took part in and their associated meanings can be charted with careful study. In the 21st century C-1933-1524 can be valued as a cultural historical touchstone, providing insight into the craft traditions, the economy, and the burial practices of Late Roman Greece.

As a final thought, when permission to study this object was given to the author in 2009, one could interpret this as yet another instance of it serving as a commodity in an exchange, with permissions granted to a young scholar in the expectation of publications of the site's material. However, given the ties that have endured between the author and Corinth Excavations, the personal relationships that have formed, and the satisfaction of working with this material, it is tempting to see

C-1933-1524 as finally having gained meaning as a gift for the first time in its biography.

Notes

[1] I thank C. Marini and L. Tzortzopoulou-Gregory for the invitation to contribute to this volume, and the anonymous reviewers for their suggestions. The Hill of Zeus material was assigned to me while a regular member of the ASCSA, with research conducted as a visiting senior associate member. My thanks to everyone at ASCSA Corinth Excavations for their support. Much of the research for this project was funded while serving as the Elisabeth Alföldi-Rosenbaum Fellow at the Canadian Institute in Greece. A full report of the Hill of Zeus pottery and context is being prepared for publication.

[2] Discussion of Late Roman lekythoi is often relegated to broader excavation reports or appears in the publication of regional conference proceedings. For Greece, a trove of reports was published in Papanikola-Bakirtzi and Kousmoulakou (2010), including reports by Chamilaki (Delion, Boiotia), Skarmoutsou (Kraneion in Corinth), and Tzavella (Athens). Excavations by Wiseman (1967a, 1967b, 1969, 1972) in Corinth's gymnasium paid particular attention to the Late Roman graves and their finds. Meleti (2013) published an extensive range of Late Roman lekythoi from an area farther east along Corinth's northern ridge. Pétridis (2012) and Poulou-Papadimitriou et al. (2012) address Late Roman graves in Greece and include discussion of the related lekythoi. This list is not extensive, but demonstrates the disparate and regional nature of the scholarship.

[3] Gosden and Marshall 1999, 169–170; see also Appadurai 1986.

[4] Gosden and Marshall 1999, 173.

[5] Ancient Corinth, Archaeological Museum of Ancient Corinth C-1933-1524, excav. 1933.

[6] Diam. base 0.065 m; max. diam. 0.074 m; H. 0.141 m; diam. rim (uneven) ca. 0.044 m.

[7] Exterior surface is yellowish red (5YR 5/6); fabric (at chipped rim) is red (approx. 2.5YR 5/8), with faint red mottling. Frequent fine subrounded black grits; few fine subrounded gray inclusions; few to frequent very fine to fine rounded and subrounded calcareous white inclusions (with few to frequent very fine to small spalling on the surface); few to frequent very fine elusive white sparkling flakes; frequent very fine to small rounded and subrounded voids. Conchoidal, slightly granular, break; soft fabric. This system of fabric description is adapted from ASCSA Corinth Excavations, originally described in Sanders 1999, 477–78.

[8] Some of the same vessels noted in the Hill of Zeus appeared in excavated contexts from the Panayia Field, dated broadly to the late-sixth and early seventh centuries; see Hammond 2015. At Athens, coins of Heraclius dated 613–615 C.E. were associated with similar

vessel shapes (if not fabrics); see Tzavella 2010, esp. pl. 1.ß for the coins. My thanks to G.D.R. Sanders for his opinion on the amount of wear on these coins, which could place them approximately a generation or two after their date of issue.

[9] The iconography of some graves and associated pottery identifies the Christian nature of the cemetery.

[10] De Waele 1935, 359; Roebuck 1951, 162.

[11] Richardson 1897, 459–60. The excavations were documented in Corinth Notebooks 1 and 1A, and published in Fowler and Stillwell 1932, 3, fig. 3. For the location of trench II in relation to later finds in the area, see Wiseman 1967b, pl. 92.

[12] Notable exceptions include brief mention of the object and/or Grave 33 in Sanders 2004, 183–84; 2005, 435; Slane and Sanders 2005, 291; Poulou-Papadimitriou et al. 2012, 383–84, fig. 3.2. The lekythos did not even receive its catalogue number, C-1933-1524, until decades after its excavation.

[13] See, e.g., Roebuck 1951, 162, pl. 15.5; Wiseman 1967a, fig. 18; 1969, figs. 9 and 11. Similar graves appear at Corinth's eastern harbor at Kenchreai; Rife et al. 2007, 154, fig. 6.

[14] Wiseman 1969, 83, Grave 77, pl. 27.e.

[15] There is some confusion in the records distinguishing Graves 33 and 34.

[16] Corinth Notebook 138, 17.

[17] Sanders 2004, 184; 2005, 436. For general discussion of funeral meals, see also Danforth 1982, 42; Alexiou 2002, 45; Rife 2012, 151.

[18] Some scholars have demonstrated that modern Greek funerary rituals have several parallels with early Christian and Byzantine practices, although an unbroken line of transmission should not necessarily be assumed; see Rife 2012, esp. 159–63, with bibliography. For the anointing of the body, see Sanders 2004, 184; 2005, 436, with specific reference to the finds from this grave.

[19] Poulou-Papadimitriou et al. 2012, 388, n. 11.

[20] For water, see Alexiou 2002, 42. For food, see Danforth 1982, 42.

[21] Although its performance at the funeral represented the culmination of this object's purpose, the new meaning it acquired was subjectively negative, and required separation from any future user and opportunity to acquire new meaning (until its excavation). For the relation between performance and meaning, see Gosden and Marshall 1999, 175.

[22] For Late Roman Corinth's regional wares, see Hammond 2015 and 2018, which expands upon Slane and Sanders 2005.

[23] For southern Argolid fabric, see Slane and Sanders (2005, 286–87), and Hammond (2015, 196–214; 2018, 675–77).

[24] C-1933-1491 and C-1933-1493 (unique lekythoi); C-1933-1507 (pitcher); and C-1933-1498, C-1933-1499, C-1933-1502, C-1933-1503, C-1933-1508, C-1933-1525, and C-1933-1531.

[25] For discussion of the kiln evidence at Kounoupi, see Munn 1985.

[26] For the role of the state in the distribution of the Late Roman Amphora 2, see Karagiorgou 2001.

[27] E.g., see Hammond 2015, nos. 134 (stamped bowl), 400 (mug), and 501 (pitcher). However, a mug (as no. 400) discovered in a grave at the Lechaion Basilica was inscribed with the (presumably) owner's name; see Pallas 1961, 173–74; Slane and Sanders 2005, 291 n. 93. See also Roberts 2002, for reused household items in Mediterranean graves of the late Classical and Hellenistic periods.

[28] See Hammond 2015, 196–214; 2018, 675–77.

[29] Thanks go to the Craft Center at Kenyon College where the author conducted experimental pottery throwing. Although the technology and raw materials differ from those of ancient potters, similar manufacturing marks were obtained utilizing basic techniques.

Works Cited

Alexiou, M. 2002. *The Ritual Lament in Greek Tradition*. 2nd ed. Revised by D. Yatromanolakis and P. Roilos. Lanham: Rowman & Littlefield.

Appadurai, A. 1986. "Introduction: Commodities and the Politics of Value." In *The Social Life of Things: Commodities in Cultural Perspective*, edited by A. Appadurai, 3–63. Cambridge: Cambridge University Press. DOI: 10.1017/ CBO9780511819582.003.

Chamilaki, K. 2010. "Ταφικά σύνολα υστερορωμαϊκών χρόνων από νεκροταφείο στο Δήλιον Βοιωτίας. Πρώτες παρατηρήσεις." In *Κεραμική της Ύστερης Αρχαιότητας από τον Ελλαδικό Χώρο (3ος–7ος αι. μ.Χ.): Επιστημονική Συνάντηση Θεσσαλονίκη, 12–16 Νοεμβρίου 2006*, edited by D. Papanikola-Bakirtzi and D. Kousmoulakou, 580–609. Thessaloniki: Αριστοτέλειο Πανεπιστήμιο Θεσσαλονίκης/Υπουργείο Πολιτισμού και Τουρισμού.

Danforth, L.M. 1982. *The Death Rituals of Rural Greece*. Princeton: Princeton University Press.

Fowler, H.N., and R. Stillwell. 1932. *Introduction, Topography, Architecture*. Corinth 1.1. Cambridge: Harvard University Press.

Gosden, C., and Y. Marshall. 1999. "The Cultural Biography of Objects." *WorldArch* 31:169–78. DOI: 10.1080/ 00438243.1999.9980439.

Hammond, M.D. 2015. "Late Roman Ceramics from the Panayia Field, Corinth (Late 4th to 7th c.): The Long-Distance, Regional and Local Wares in Their Economic, Social and Historical Contexts." Ph.D. diss., University of Missouri.

———. 2018. "Late Roman (late 4th to 7th c.) Ceramics from the

Panayia Field in Corinth, Greece: The Local and Regional Networks of a Globalized City." *RCRFActa* 45:675–84.

Karagiorgou, O. 2001. "Late Roman 2 Amphora: A Container for the Military *Annona* on the Danubian Border?" In *Economy and Exchange in the East Mediterranean during Late Antiquity: Proceedings of a Conference at Somerville College, Oxford, 29th May, 1999*, edited by S. Kingsley and M. Decker, 129–66. Oxford: Oxbow.

Meleti, P. 2013. "Παλαιοχριστιανικό νεκροταφείο στην Αρχαία Κορίνθο." In *The Corinthia and the Northeast Peloponnese: Topography and History from Prehistoric Times until the End of Antiquity; Proceedings of the International Conference Organized by the Directorate of Prehistoric and Classical Antiquities, the LZ' Ephorate of Prehistoric and Classical Antiquities and the German Archaeological Institute, Athens, Held at Loutraki, March 26–29, 2009*, edited by K. Kissas and W.-D. Niemeier, 161–67. Athenaia 4. Munich: Hirmer Verlag.

Munn, M.L.Z. 1985. "A Late Roman Kiln Site in the Hermionid, Greece (abstract)." *AJA* 89:342–43.

Pallas, D. 1961. "Ανασκαφή της Βασιλικής εν Λεχαίω." *Prakt* (1956):164–78.

Papanikola-Bakirtzi, D., and D. Kousmoulakou, eds. 2010. *Κεραμική της Ύστερης Αρχαιότητας από τον Ελλαδικό Χώρο (3ος–7ος αι. μ.Χ.): Επιστημονική Συνάντηση Θεσσαλονίκη, 12–16 Νοεμβρίου 2006*. 2 vols. Thessaloniki: Αριστοτέλειο Πανεπιστήμιο Θεσσαλονίκης/ Υπουργείο Πολιτισμού και Τουρισμού.

Pétridis, P. 2012. "Céramique protobyzantine *intentionnellement* ou *accessoirement* funéraire?" In *Atti del IX Congresso Internazionale sulla Ceramica Medievale nel Mediterraneo: Venezia, Scuola Grande dei Carmini Auditorium Santa Margherita 23–27 novembre 2009*, edited by S. Gelichi, 423–28. Firenze: All'Insegna del Giglio.

Poulou-Papadimitriou, N., E. Tzavella, and J. Ott. 2012. "Burial Practices in Byzantine Greece: Archaeological Evidence and Methodological Problems for Its Interpretation." In *Rome, Constantinople and Newly-Converted Europe: Archaeological and Historical Evidence*, vol. 1, edited by M. Salamon, M. Wołoszyn, A. Musin, and P. Špehar, 377–428. Krakow, Leipzig, Rzeszów, and Warsaw: Instytut Archeologii i Etnologii Polskiej akademii nauk/Frühzeit Ostmitteleuropas.

Richardson, R.B. 1897. "The Excavations at Corinth in 1896." *AJA* 1:455–80. DOI: 10.2307/496780.

Roberts, H.S. 2002. "Pots for the Living, Pots for the Dead: Were Pots Purpose-Made for the Funeral or Reused? Can Inscriptions Throw Light on the Problem?" In *Pots for the Living, Pots for the Dead*, edited by A. Rathje, M. Nielsen, and

B.B. Rasmussen, 9–32. Acta Hyperborea 9. Copenhagen: Museum Tusculanum Press.

Roebuck, C. 1951. *The Asklepieion and Lerna.* Corinth 14. Princeton: American School of Classical Studies at Athens.

Rife, J.L. 2012. *The Roman and Byzantine Graves and Human Remains.* Isthmia 9. Princeton: American School of Classical Studies at Athens.

Rife, J.L., M.M. Morison, A. Barbet, R.K. Dunn, D.H. Ubelaker, and F. Monier. 2007. "Life and Death at a Port in Roman Greece: The Kenchreai Cemetery Project, 2002–2006." *Hesperia* 76:143–81. DOI: 10.2972/hesp.76.1.143.

Sanders, G.D.R. 1999. "A Late Roman Bath at Corinth: Excavations in the Panayia Field, 1995–1996." *Hesperia* 68:441–80. DOI: 10.2307/148411.

———. 2004. "Problems in Interpreting Rural and Urban Settlement in Southern Greece, AD 365–700." In *Landscapes of Change: Rural Evolutions in Late Antiquity and the Early Middle Ages*, edited by N. Christie, 163–93. Aldershot: Ashgate.

———. 2005. "Archaeological Evidence for Early Christianity and the End of Hellenic Religion in Corinth." In *Urban Religion in Roman Corinth: Interdisciplinary Approaches*, edited by D.N. Schowalter and S.J. Friesen, 419–42. Harvard Theological Studies 53. Cambridge: Harvard University Press.

Skarmoutsou, K. 2010. "Κεραμική από παλαιοχριστιανικό νεκροταφείο περιοχής Κρανείου–Αρχαίας Κορίνθου." In *Κεραμική της Ύστερης Αρχαιότητας από τον Ελλαδικό Χώρο (3ος–7ος αι. μ.Χ.): Επιστημονική Συνάντηση Θεσσαλονίκη, 12–16 Νοεμβρίου 2006*, edited by D. Papanikola-Bakirtzi and D. Kousmoulakou, 712–42. Thessaloniki: Αριστοτέλειο Πανεπιστήμιο Θεσσαλονίκης/Υπουργείο Πολιτισμού και Τουρισμού.

Slane, K.W., and G.D.R. Sanders. 2005. "Corinth: Late Roman Horizons." *Hesperia* 74:243–97. DOI: 10.1353/hes.2005.0007.

Tzavella, E. 2010. "Κεραμική από αθηναϊκούς τάφους του τέλους της Αρχαιότητας και οι μαρτυρίες της για τον 7ο αι. στην Αττική." In *Κεραμική της Ύστερης Αρχαιότητας από τον Ελλαδικό Χώρο (3ος–7ος αι. μ.Χ.): Επιστημονική Συνάντηση Θεσσαλονίκη, 12–16 Νοεμβρίου 2006*, edited by D. Papanikola-Bakirtzi and D. Kousmoulakou, 649–70. Thessaloniki: Αριστοτέλειο Πανεπιστήμιο Θεσσαλονίκης/Υπουργείο Πολιτισμού και Τουρισμού.

de Waele, F.J. 1935. "The Fountain of Lerna and the Early Christian Cemetery at Corinth." *AJA* 39:352–59. DOI: 10.2307/498622.

Wiseman, J. 1967a. "Excavations at Corinth, The Gymnasium Area, 1965." *Hesperia* 36:13–41. DOI: 10.2307/147615.

———. 1967b. "Excavations at Corinth the Gymnasium Area, 1966." *Hesperia* 36:402–28. DOI: 10.2307/147370.

———. 1969. "Excavations in Corinth, The Gymnasium Area, 1967–1968." *Hesperia* 38:64–106. DOI: 10.2307/147640.

———. 1972. "The Gymnasium Area at Corinth, 1969–1970." *Hesperia* 41:1–42. DOI: 10.2307/147475.

The Circulation of Achilles's Shield on the Berthouville Pitchers

David Petrain

Abstract

A pair of first-century C.E. silver pitchers found near the village of Berthouville in northwest France carry a cycle of images depicting scenes from the Trojan War whose iconography and significance are ripe for reappraisal now that the pitchers, along with the rest of the Berthouville treasure, have recently undergone conservation and cleaning. I reevaluate the identity of several figures featured in the scenes and argue that the pitchers are constructing a narrative about the famous shield of Achilles—newly prominent thanks to gilding revealed by the conservation—and how it passed into his possession and then after his death was awarded as a prize to Odysseus. By rewriting the saga of Achilles as a story about the circulation of an exquisitely wrought object that bestows prestige on a succession of owners, the pitchers encourage reflection on their own status as carriers of value and on the importance of the itinerary they themselves have traversed. The shield with its contested ownership becomes an emblem of how Quintus Domitius Tutus, the dedicator whose name is inscribed on both pitchers, appropriates and transfers the cultural cachet of Greek epic, giving it new meaning in the context of a Gallo-Roman sanctuary to Mercury.

IN 1830, A FARMER WORKING HIS FIELD NEAR THE SMALL village of Berthouville in northwest France struck a tile about half a foot below the soil, and found underneath it a deposit of approximately 90 pieces of ancient Roman silver. The entire treasure was purchased shortly thereafter for the Cabinet des Médailles of what would become the Bibliothèque nationale de France, in Paris, where it is held to this day. Among the objects that make up the Berthouville treasure are a pair of silver pitchers decorated in repoussé work, whose necks and bodies depict scenes from the Trojan War, with a particular focus on the life and death of the hero Achilles. All of these objects, pitchers included, traveled overseas for the first time in 2010 to the Getty Museum in Los Angeles, where they underwent a four-year program of cleaning, conservation, and study that removed tarnish, revealed new details of the reliefs that adorn many of the vessels, and uncovered traces of gilding more extensive than had been visible previously. In their newly restored state, then, the two pitchers and their images of Achilles's life are ripe for a reappraisal.[1]

In this study, I will offer a reinterpretation of the iconography of several scenes on the pitchers, and will argue that the story they offer encourages us to focus not just on the life of Achilles, but on the vicissitudes of the famous shield made for him by the god Hephaestus, and how it passed into and out of the hero's possession. I will further argue that we are meant to link the shield with the pitchers themselves, and to see in its fortunes an emblem of the value and prestige that the pitchers too promise to bestow upon their owners. By presenting the shield of Achilles as an object whose circulation among owners and incidents is constitutive of its meaning, the pitchers lay a claim to their own history and assert the importance of the itineraries they themselves have traversed.[2]

Context and Dating

The objects that make up the Berthouville treasure seem to have been deposited deliberately just within the precinct of an extraurban sanctuary to Mercury. Inscriptions on several pieces suggest that most if not all of them were dedications to the god. Campaigns of excavation undertaken in the 19th century revealed that the sanctuary went through two phases of construction before being destroyed in a fire, but it is difficult to date the phases or to determine when precisely the silver was deposited. The balance of evidence suggests that the sanctuary's first phase corresponds roughly to the first and second centuries C.E., and that the deposit occurred in the late second or early third century C.E. Why the silver was stored away like this remains unclear.[3]

The period of the deposit provides only a terminus ante quem for the objects themselves. Some seem to be of Gallic manufacture and could date from the second century C.E.[4] Our pitchers, however, belong to a well-defined group of nine vessels dedicated by one Quintus Domitius Tutus, named in inscriptions on each of them. The dedications of Tutus stand out for their elaborate decoration and their tendency to occur in pairs, like our pitchers. Because they resemble metal vessels from the Bay of Naples area that predate Vesuvius's eruption, the general consensus is that both the pitchers and the majority of Tutus's other dedications were created in the first century C.E., in Italy. They would not originally have been conceived as dedications but rather as items for display or use at a banquet. Our pitchers thus have a complex life history, traveling from Italy to Gaul before being repurposed as dedications to a local god.[5] We will return to how this itinerary may inflect a reading of the pitchers' imagery in the final section.

Description

Each pitcher consists of a concave neck that is triangular in cross-section, an ovoid body, and a low foot.[6] A high, curving handle rises from the back of each neck and attaches to the body just above an appliqué element in the form of a mask. The neck and handle create for each pitcher a central axis, that is, an obverse and a reverse defined respectively by the neck with the pitcher's spout at its peak, and the attachment of the handle to the body at the appliqué mask.

The necks and bodies are covered by figural decoration in repoussé work. Each neck depicts an altar at the front approached by two figures on either side. Each body features two scenes arrayed continuously along its ovoid surface, with one scene more extensive and the other slightly more compressed. To facilitate the presentation of all this material, I offer at the outset a conspectus of the images on each pitcher in tabular format. In the two rows, I name the vessels *Pitcher A* and *Pitcher B* purely for convenience; in the columns, *Body₁* refers to the more extensive scene on each pitcher's body and *Body₂* to the more compressed one.

Table 1. Conspectus of images on the Berthouville pitchers.

	Neck	$Body_1$	$Body_2$
Pitcher A	Theft of Palladium	Mourning over Patroclus	Ransom of Hector
Pitcher B	Doloneia	Dragging of Hector	Death of Achilles

As the conspectus shows, the four scenes on the bodies focus on Achilles through the interconnected deaths of Patroclus, Hector, and Achilles himself. The necks feature two exploits of Odysseus that are less closely linked to the story of Achilles's life below but nonetheless reinforce its themes, as will emerge from the analysis to follow. To begin with the necks:[7] that of Pitcher A shows Diomedes and Odysseus in the act of stealing from Troy the Palladium, the miniature statue of Athena that guaranteed the city's safety and according to prophecy had to be stolen before Troy could fall. As often on these pitchers, Odysseus may be identified by the conical hat he wears, his characteristic *pilos*. The neck of Pitcher B features Odysseus in his *pilos* again, facing a figure who is perhaps the Trojan spy Dolon, identified by his wolf skin: this will be a scene from the Doloneia of *Iliad* book 10, an episode in which Odysseus and Diomedes intercept Dolon as he attempts to reconnoiter the Greek camp at night under camouflage.[8]

The scenes on the bodies are considerably more elaborate and interact differently with the obverse–reverse axis of each pitcher.[9] On Pitcher A, the scenes are static and centered on the main axis, with figures arranged symmetrically around a central element, the corpse of a deceased hero. The front of the pitcher shows the Greek chieftains mourning Patroclus, slain by Hector while he was disguised in his companion Achilles's armor (fig. 1). A beardless, nude Achilles sits to the left of Patroclus and bends his head toward him; behind Achilles, Odysseus in his *pilos* buries his face in his hand (fig. 2). Eight other Greek warriors, some clothed and some nude, sit or stand on rocks at various levels around the corpse; one of these, bald and older than the others, rests his hand and elbow on a shield (fig. 3).

On the back of Pitcher A, we see the ransom of Hector, slain by Achilles in reprisal for Patroclus's death (fig. 4). A massive set of scales stands in the middle; the mask below the handle attachment seems almost to hang from its central support. One pan of the scales holds the body of Hector, the other a vessel that represents the ransom brought by the five Trojans who stand to the right in attitudes of lamentation. Opposite this group on the left, Achilles sits in a chair with one foot on a stool, his hand rested on the back of his shield. Four Greeks attend him, among them Odysseus, who stands in front of him with his back to the scales and is identified by his *pilos*. The scene is familiar from book 24 of the *Iliad*, but the motif of weighing Hector's body against the ransom seems rather to go back to Aeschylus, who dramatized it in

Fig. 1 (opposite). Front view of Pitcher A (Paris, Bibliothèque nationale de France, Département des Monnaies, Médailles et Antiques, inv. 56.4; source of all images of Pitcher A: gallica.bnf.fr / Bibliothèque nationale de France).

32

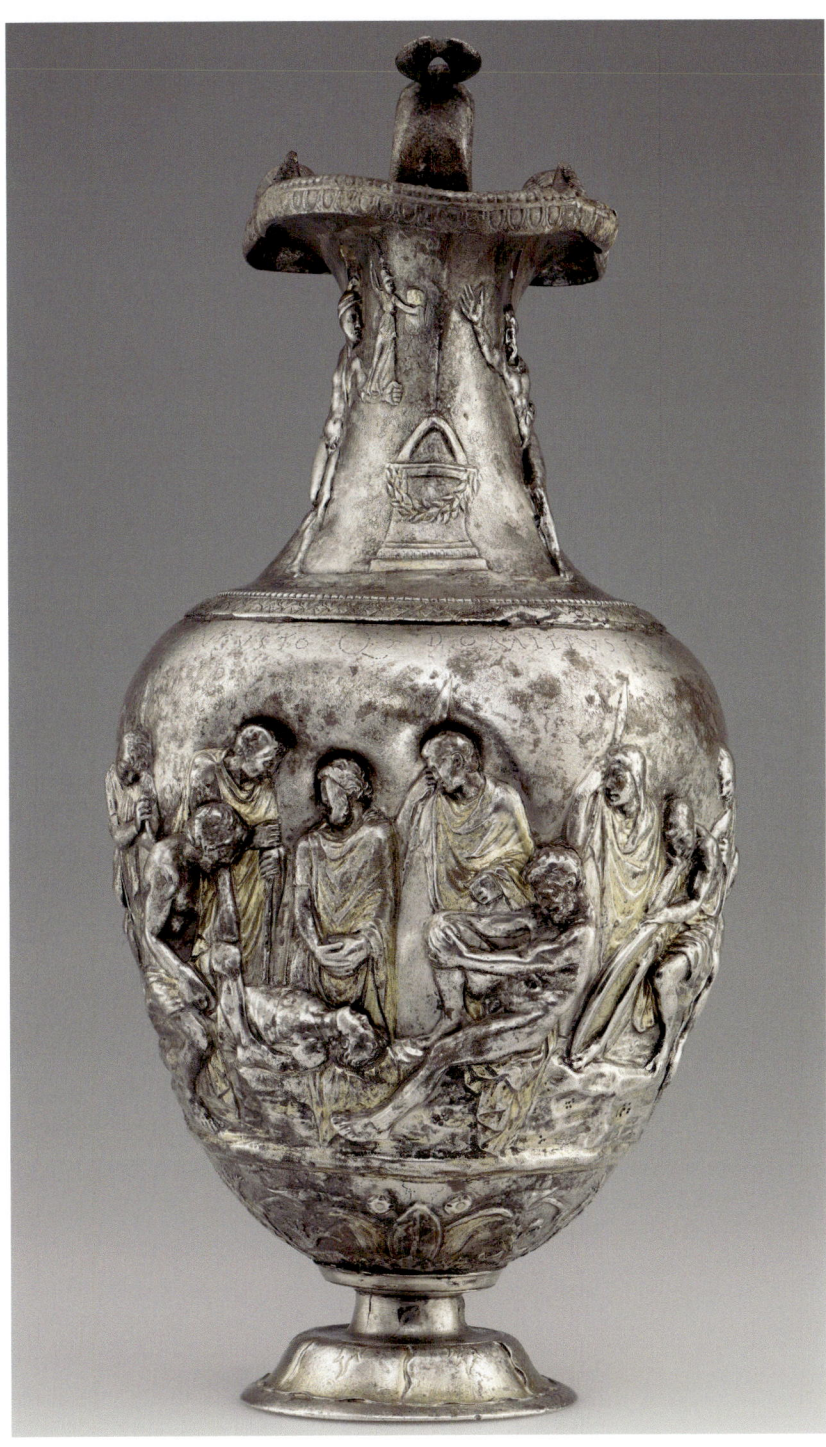

Fig. 2. Side view of Pitcher A.

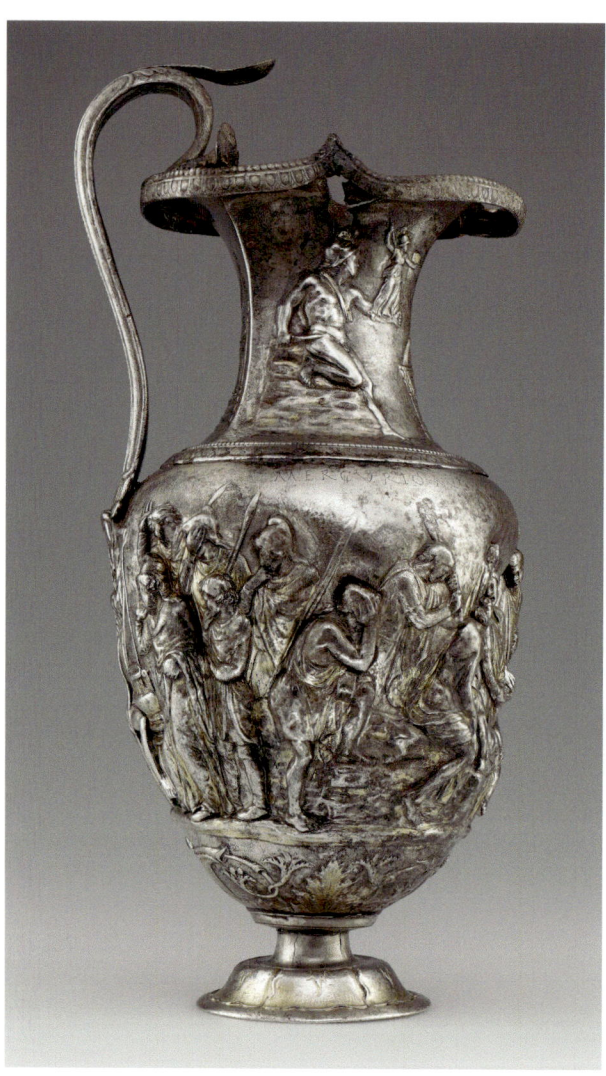

his lost play *The Phrygians*. The motif is a rarity in ancient art.[10]

On Pitcher B, a wall, whose masonry, crenelations, and towers run continuously along the body of the pitcher, locates the actions depicted just outside the city of Troy. The scenes are not centered on the pitcher's main axis, which rather marks points of transition between them. The mask on the reverse, for instance, hovers at a boundary created by the centrifugal movement of two warriors with their backs to one another who belong to separate episodes (fig. 5). Just below the mask, the extended leg of a Greek warrior rushing forward initiates

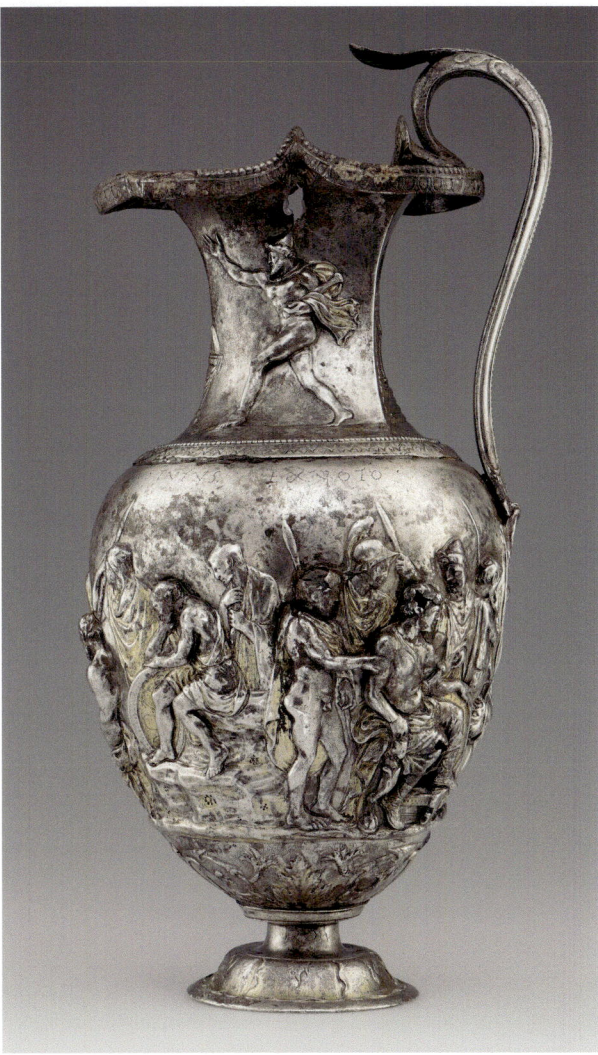

Fig. 3. Side view of Pitcher A.

the violent motion to the right that characterizes both scenes and guides us around the pitcher. As we follow this rightward motion, we meet first with Achilles in his chariot (fig. 6). He drags the bound corpse of Hector behind him while his charioteer urges the horses onward, an episode that precedes the ransom scene of Pitcher A in the chronology of the narrative. Three Greek warriors follow the chariot on foot, and from the wall, Priam and a woman who may be Hecuba or Andromache extend their hands in horror. Achilles raises his shield over his head to protect himself from two Trojan warriors who aim spears at him from the wall. On the obverse

Fig. 4. Back view of Pitcher A.

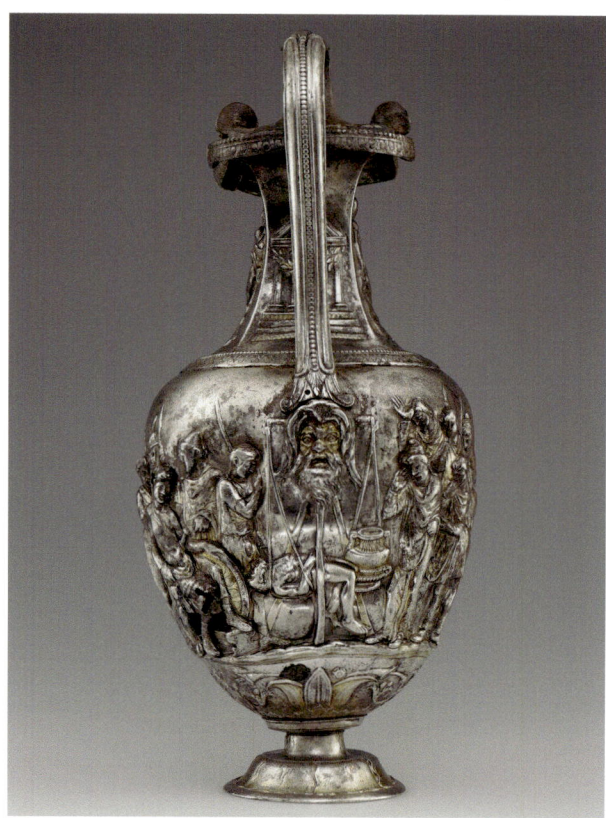

below the pitcher's spout, another Trojan has fallen on his back underneath Achilles's horses (fig. 7), and the lower half of his body extends into the next scene: the death of Achilles.

In this scene (fig. 8), Achilles has been felled by the arrow protruding from his ankle; he crumples to the ground with his shield dropped behind him. A warrior attempts to lift him while protecting the body with his shield extended overhead: this must be Ajax. To the left, three Trojans press on the attack. These are balanced by three Greek warriors in addition to Ajax. One is just visible in the background above Ajax's shield, as a helmeted head and raised arm with sword, while a second has fallen to the ground just behind Ajax. The third strides to the left to join the fight with his sword raised, in a motion that checks the otherwise rightward onslaught of the images on Pitcher B, as if to bring them to a conclusion. And finally, in the space between this third figure and Ajax, there is a winged figure of Victory, who flies to the right with a palm

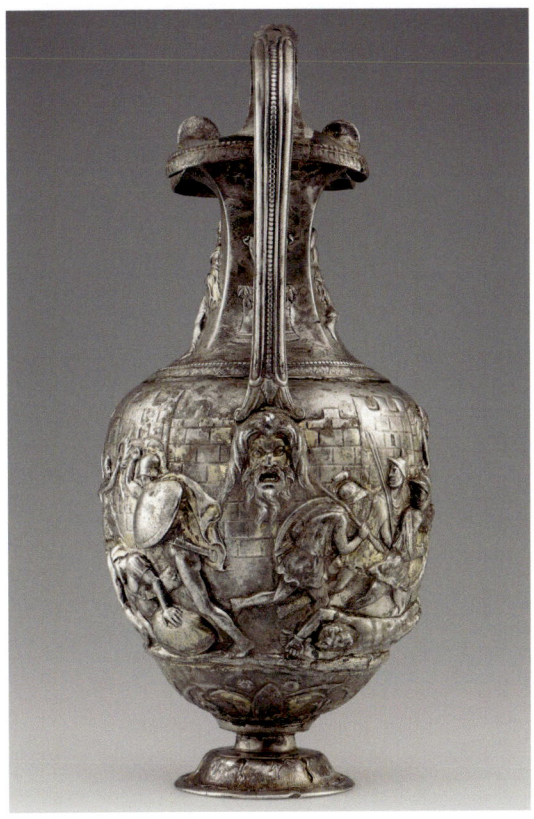

Fig. 5. Back view of Pitcher B (Paris, Bibliothèque nationale de France, Département des Monnaies, Médailles et Antiques, inv. 56.5; source of all images of Pitcher B: gallica.bnf.fr / Bibliothèque nationale de France).

frond in one hand and a wreath in the other that she seems to extend toward the striding Greek warrior.

Anticipating Victory

Discussions of the narrative cycle on the bodies of our pitchers have tended to focus on the intricate web of cause and effect, the reversals of fortune and alternations of success and defeat, that their selection of scenes highlights.[11] This must indeed be part of the meaning the pitchers held for their viewers, but the figure of Victory adds a key element to the story that has not yet been fully appreciated.

Victory's presence at the death of Achilles is unexpected. While the fight over Achilles's corpse is not a common subject in ancient art, this is the only extant version of the scene that includes her participation.[12] The uniqueness of her appearance here alone might suggest that she requires interpretation and that her significance is not immediately obvious. Such at

Fig. 6. Side view of Pitcher B.

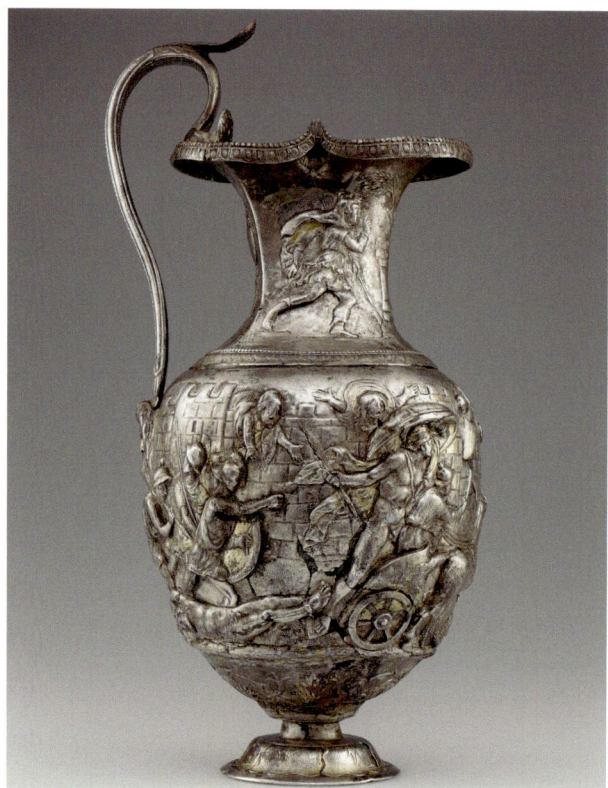

least is the impression given by the divergent explanations that modern discussions have offered to account for her. One idea is that she has been misplaced: images of Achilles dragging the corpse of Hector sometimes feature a Victory in front of his chariot; perhaps our Victory really belongs to the prior scene.[13] But such an unmotivated displacement seems unlikely—How could viewers have understood that she belongs not among the figures who surround her, but with the chariot on the other side of the pitcher? Another suggestion is that Victory is leading the Trojans forward and signals their triumph over Achilles.[14] This seems difficult visually, however: though Victory *does* move in the same direction as the three Trojans who open the scene, she is separated from them by Achilles and Ajax and is flying among the Greeks. As for the narrative context, the *Greeks* are the victors in the battle over Achilles's corpse, rescuing it along with the hero's arms and, in at least one account, killing many Trojans besides.[15] Achilles's death is difficult to read as a straightforward Trojan victory.

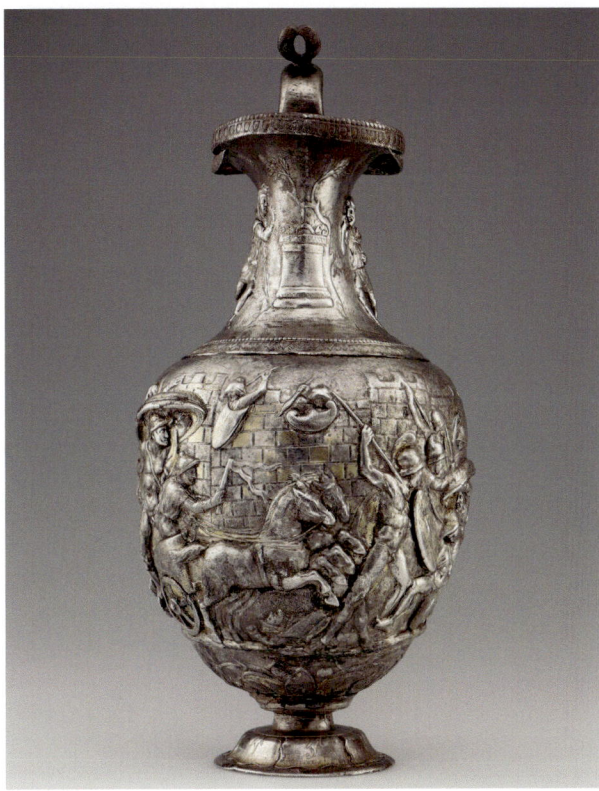

Fig. 7. Front view of Pitcher B.

In any case, the battle is ongoing and victory has not yet been attained. Thus, in this final scene of Achilles's life, we have an element that asks us to consider what happens next. Victory is the only divinity depicted on the pitchers, and I argue that she appears here because, as the divine guarantor of successful outcomes, she is able to gesture toward the future in a way no human character could. The stroke of genius on the part of the artisans of the pitchers is to include her at this final moment as a way of enlisting viewers' active participation in extending the story forward, beyond what the pitchers can show. We are meant to consider how her presence might be justified by the consequences of Achilles's death.

Different viewers may fill in Victory's prolepsis in different ways, and it may not be necessary to insist on a single interpretation. Rather, her role in the narrative economy of the pitchers is to broaden the scope of the limited number of images they offer by stimulating a process of supplementation, as viewers try to identify which victory she might refer to. The most recent catalogue of the Berthouville treasure

Fig. 8. Side view of Pitcher B.

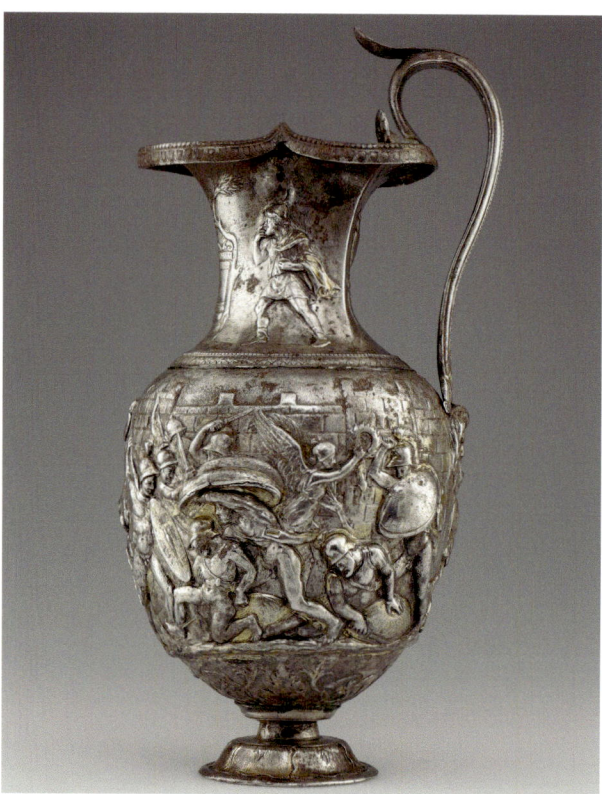

follows her lead when it suggests that the Victory attending Achilles's death simply indicates that the Greeks will eventually win, despite the setback of losing Achilles: she is flying toward their side, after all.[16] This is reasonable—some viewers may well have explained the significance of her presence in this way—but I argue that her reference is potentially more pointed, and that the version of Achilles's life constructed by the pitchers encourages us to have a more specific victory in mind.

Let us take a closer look at the striding Greek warrior Victory seems to approach. In textual accounts of the death of Achilles, two warriors' involvement is regularly signaled: that of Ajax, who lifts the corpse, and of Odysseus, who provides cover while he does so. The two play this role as early as archaic epic.[17] Among visual representations, an early first-century C.E. version of the scene featured on the *Tabula Capitolina*, the best preserved of the *Tabulae Iliacae*, seems to be the earliest extant example that explicitly picks up Odysseus's involvement:[18] Achilles collapses before the Scaean Gate;

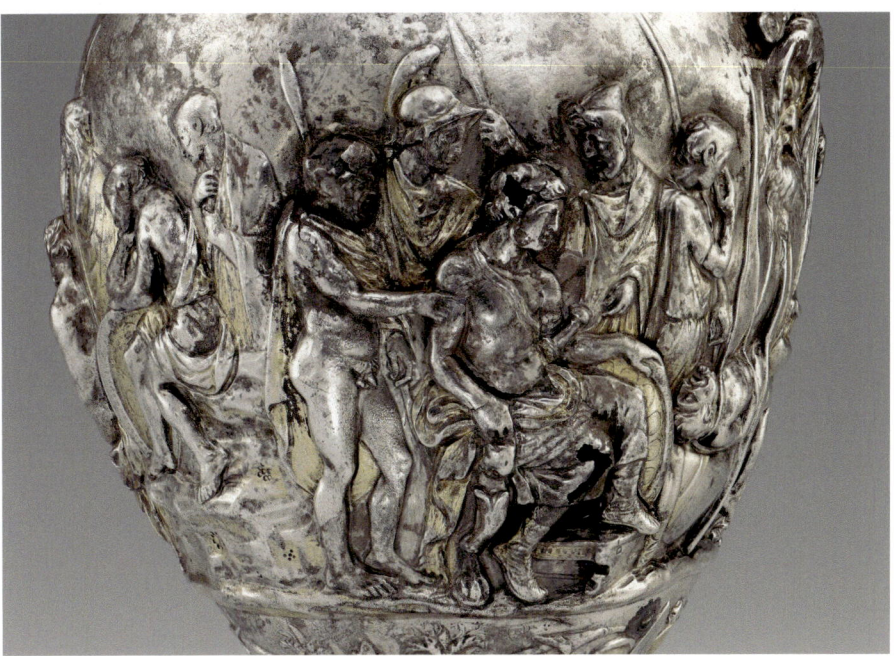

Ajax approaches from the right to shield him and Odysseus follows behind (all three figures are labeled). The detail of Odysseus striding behind Ajax, and the emphasis on the scene's architectural setting, parallel the approximately contemporary depiction on our pitcher.

Fig. 9. Side view of Pitcher A, detail.

In his analysis of Achilles's death on Pitcher B, K. Lehmann-Hartleben finds Odysseus among the figures but surprisingly enough identifies him with the fallen Greek warrior behind Ajax; Kossatz-Deissmann registers this identification in her description of the scene for *LIMC* and judges it plausible (*erwägenswert*).[19] But there are reasons for doubt. If Odysseus has fallen, it is hard to see how he can play his traditional role of offering protection to Ajax. In addition, the fallen warrior is clad in armor, but throughout the scenes on the pitchers, the heroes who serve as their protagonists tend to be distinguished from rank-and-file soldiers by their nudity.[20] The nudity of the striding figure behind Ajax should therefore be a sign that he is a person of note, and on the basis of the parallel from the *Tabula Capitolina*, this is the figure whom I would identify as Odysseus. An additional clue in support of this identification may come from the pitcher's neck just above, which features Odysseus striding toward Dolon in a similar posture and with the same arm raised, and thereby

41

encourages viewers to connect the two figures.[21] Although Odysseus wears his *pilos* on the neck above and in his other appearances on the pitchers, and is not always distinguished by heroic nudity, the martial context motivates his different costume, with a helmet rather than the customary *pilos*, at the fight over Achilles's corpse, and his nudity indexes the fact that here he steps to the forefront of the action—no longer a mere attendant of Achilles as in the other scenes on the bodies, but a protagonist in his own right.

The identification of the striding figure as Odysseus may help us to sharpen our understanding of Victory's presence in the scene. If Victory is moving to crown Odysseus, and thereby invites viewers to think of a success specifically involving him, it is not hard to imagine what that success would be. For Ajax and Odysseus, a major consequence of the retrieval of Achilles's body will be their quarrel over which of them should be given Achilles's armor and shield.[22] I suggest that it is Odysseus's victory in this contest, and more specifically his winning of the shield, that Victory points to as she flies away from Ajax and toward the figure who brings the scenes on the body of Pitcher B to an end.

The Cycle of the Shield

To corroborate the possible allusion here to the dispute over Achilles's arms and shield, I note that the artisans have taken pains to depict the hero's shield in all four scenes on the pitchers' bodies. As Achilles collapses in death on Pitcher B (fig. 8), his shield has fallen to the ground just behind him. He raises it above his head during the dragging of Hector on the same pitcher (fig. 6). We see the shield in the ransom scene of Pitcher A too (fig. 4), resting on the ground with its back to the viewer as Achilles rests his hand on it. Though only part of the shield emerges from behind Achilles's leg, it is worth noting how carefully it has been characterized. Its ungilded silver rim bears a repeating decorative element; within this rim, the gilded back shows the ends of petal-like forms that we might imagine radiating from the center (fig. 9).

Finally, a shield is featured conspicuously in the other scene on Pitcher A, the mourning over Patroclus, as the only piece of armor carried among the assembled Greek warriors. The shield rests on the ground while a figure leans his elbow and hand on its rim (fig. 3). Its decoration resembles that of the shield held by Achilles in the ransom scene, with the same silver rim engraved with a repeating motif, and gilded back adorned by shapes in the form of petals. When the pitcher is viewed from certain angles (fig. 9), the two shields may be seen at once and look like mirror images of one another, the right half at the ransom scene complemented by the left half at the scene of mourning. This latter shield, of course, is held not by Achilles, who sits near Patroclus's body, but rather by an older, balding figure looking on from a distance away.

Discussions of this scene tend not to devote much attention to the shield, but I argue that it plays a crucial role in the event depicted and is meant to be identified with the shield held by Achilles in the following three scenes.[23] In book 19 of the *Iliad*, Thetis presents Achilles with his new armor shortly before the Greeks begin their lamentation over Patroclus, and a handful of images from the archaic period likewise connect the mourning scene explicitly with the delivery of the armor.[24] The *Tabulae Iliacae* may help us forge a closer link: while they do not include the mourning scene, they portray an episode that occurs shortly after, when Achilles puts on his new armor, and in that episode they include a male figure who assists at the arming, and whom the *Tabula Capitolina* labels as Phoenix.[25] On Pitcher A, the advanced age of the figure holding the shield makes it reasonable to suppose that the shield is not his, that he will not himself be carrying it into battle: I suspect this is the aged Phoenix as well, holding his charge's shield in a role not dissimilar to the one he plays on the *Tabulae*.[26] Regardless of his identity, it makes iconographic and narrative sense that the shield he holds is the same as its visual counterpart that rests by Achilles in the ransom scene, created by Hephaestus to replace the shield Patroclus lost and delivered to Achilles moments before he and the Greek chiefs begin their lamentation.

The artisans of the pitchers have selected scenes from Achilles's life in such a way that the four vignettes also give us a full biography, as it were, of his shield. We see it from the moment it enters his possession to the moment of his death, in which the figure of Victory advances to crown Odysseus as its eventual new owner. The life of Achilles has been rewritten as a story about the circulation and changing ownership of an object with a complex and significant life history.

An Epic of Objects

The shield's appearances in each of the four vignettes dramatize the paramount importance of an exquisitely wrought object that accumulates meaning as it passes through the different phases of its itinerary. There is no attempt to reproduce the shield's decoration as described in Homer's ecphrasis because for the pitchers, I suggest, what matters is not the distinctiveness of the shield's images but the extent of its circulation: where it comes from, where it is going, and who possesses it. This prominence given to the shield and its movements suggests the possibility of reading it as a mise en abyme for the objects it adorns. Links between the pitchers and the shield, both material and thematic, are near to hand: the pitchers are made of the same precious metals as the shield, and they too change hands and contribute to the prestige of their owners partly by virtue of the images they carry. The very abundance of their imagery also suggests a connection with Hephaestus's creation, the work of figural art par excellence. An association between shield and pitchers would invest with an epic grandeur the vessels themselves and the transactions in which they take part. Their version of the Troy saga even seems to promise their owners a role analogous to that of an epic hero, as victorious possessors on a par with Odysseus. More broadly, the shield's story exemplifies the kind of attention to which the pitchers lay claim for themselves and their own circulation.

Once we have noticed that Achilles's shield could be taken as a mise en abyme for the pitchers themselves, another distinctive aspect of their iconography falls into place, namely that they seem to introduce significant objects into the narrative at every opportunity. The motif of weighing Hector's corpse makes especial sense in the way it turns the hero's body into a fungible commodity that can be measured against a gilded silver vessel—an even closer match to the pitchers themselves. And consider the scene on the neck of Pitcher A, with Odysseus and Diomedes stealing the Palladium. This vignette is about the transportation of another small, portable object, the statue of Athena whose movement will change the tide of the war and grant victory to its possessors. The entire pictorial cycle of the pitchers converts the epic tradition into a sophisticated argument for the importance of attending to objects and the meanings they carry.

Parallel Itineraries of Pitchers and Shield

We cannot know whether the dedicator of the pitchers, Quintus Domitius Tutus, had anything to do with designing their self-reflexive take on the Trojan War. But his action of dedicating them in northwest Gaul necessarily entangles them and their imagery in a new, multilayered set of associations. The inscriptions that record this action, added in dotted letters just below the neck of each vessel, read as follows:

> MERCURIO AUGUSTO Q. DOMITIUS
> TUTUS EX VOTO
> To Augustan Mercury, Quintus Domitius Tutus
> in fulfillment of his vow.

With Mercury's epithet *Augusto*, Quintus links the local god with the imperial center;[27] with his three names, he advertises his own status as a Roman citizen. Yet his cognomen, Tutus, may tell us more. It looks like the Latin word for "safe," but it has been argued recently that the name is in fact derived from the Celtic word for "people," *toutu*,[28] in the same way that many of the cognomina attested in inscriptions from the Berthouville treasure are names of Celtic origin, outfitted with Latin morphology and inflection.[29]

Tutus, then, is a Romanized Celt, the dedicator of pitchers that were transferred from Italy in the center of the empire to a sanctuary on its periphery. Once objects of display, the pitchers acquire an additional significance as honoring a local version of Mercury. Their new setting may even valorize further the figure of Odysseus depicted in their reliefs. The hero would now serve not just as the image of a victorious possessor, but as an epic model and precedent for the long journey to the edges of the known world that the pitchers, and perhaps Tutus himself, have also undertaken. Because Odysseus was one of Mercury's favorites, his prominence on the pitchers could even be taken as a compliment to the god and a hint at the divine favor that Tutus hopes to secure through his dedication. Be that as it may, the pitchers illustrate how such transfers of cultural cachet are possible as they adapt the epic tradition to the interests of the owners and honorees of the precious silver vessels. By suggesting an analogy between the objects themselves and Achilles's divinely crafted shield, the image cycle of the two Berthouville pitchers creates a connection that highlights their own itinerary, and redounds to the credit of the artists, the owners, and indeed everyone privileged enough to interact with the pitchers—even Mercury himself.

Notes

I presented versions of this chapter at the 2023 annual meeting of the AIA and at a seminar held in honor of my teacher, Gloria Ferrari Pinney, who sadly passed away in September. My thanks go to both audiences for their feedback, and especially to Gloria for her sage advice and support over the years; I dedicate this chapter to her memory. I am also grateful to the editors of this volume, the editorial board, and the anonymous reviewers for helpful comments that have improved the chapter and given me much to think about for future work on the pitchers.

[1] See Lapatin 2014, 1–3 for a brief synopsis of the conservation work at the Getty; see Sánchez and Lansing Maish 2014 for a fuller report.

[2] My thinking on the pitchers is influenced by recent work on object biographies and itineraries; see, e.g., Bauer (2019) and Canevaro (2019, esp. 230–31).

[3] Avisseau-Broustet and Colonna 2017b offers a detailed account of the discovery of the treasure and the subsequent excavations; see also Nuber 1974 on the date of the deposit. Fauduet 2017 places the sanctuary and its architecture in the context of similar sanctuaries throughout Roman Gaul.

[4] See the cautious discussion at Avisseau-Broustet and Colonna 2017b, 49–54.

[5] On the dedications of Tutus and the likelihood that they were originally conceived as display pieces rather than dedications, see Avisseau-Broustet and Colonna 2017b, 44–48; and Dondin-Payre 2017, 59.

[6] The most reliable descriptions of the two pitchers are now the catalog entries by Cécile Colonna at Lapatin 2014, 52–57; and Avisseau-Broustet and Colonna 2017a, 208–15 (more detailed), both with bibliography. The earlier description by Babelon (1916, 81–87) is still valuable. Lehmann-Hartleben 1938 and Picard 1948 offer detailed analyses of the pitchers' reliefs that have influenced subsequent treatments.

[7] Because the scenes on the necks wrap around the pitchers, they can be viewed fully only by rotating the vessels and are difficult to make out in any one image. For the neck of Pitcher A, see figs. 1–4, and for that of Pitcher B, figs. 5–8. I plan to discuss the necks and their iconography more fully in a future article.

[8] This scene is the only one whose identification is controversial. Picard (1948, 102–5) suggests instead that it shows Odysseus and Diomedes on Lemnos at the altar near which Philoctetes was wounded, though his argument has not won any supporters (cf.

LIMC Dolon 6 and Avisseau-Broustet and Colonna 2017a, 212).

[9] For a good formal analysis of how the scenes are disposed on each pitcher, see Lehmann-Hartleben 1938, 85.

[10] On the motif of the weighing and its appearance in visual representations, see Kossatz-Deissmann 1981, 147–48, 159; 2009, 14–15.

[11] E.g., Babelon 1916, 81; Lehmann-Hartleben 1938, 88; Avisseau-Broustet and Colonna 2017a, 212.

[12] See *LIMC* Achilleus 848–59 for the relevant images, with Kossatz-Deissmann's discussion (1981, 185).

[13] Avisseau-Broustet and Colonna 2017a, 212 ("peut-être la Victoire, qui ici est insérée dans la scène de la mort d'Achille, est-elle en fait liée à la précédente"). Cf. Kossatz-Deissmann 1981, 146, along with her discussion of our pitcher's version at *LIMC* Achilleus 616.

[14] Lehmann-Hartleben 1938, 97; Kossatz-Deissmann at *LIMC* Achilleus 856 ("[Nike] überbringt nicht den Griechen den Sieg, sondern läuft den Trojanern voran").

[15] See Quintus of Smyrna, *Posthomerica* 3.212–350.

[16] Avisseau-Broustet and Colonna 2017a, 212 ("On peut aussi voir la Victoire partant vers la droite comme une désignation, par anticipation, du camp qui sera finalement vainqueur de la guerre, celui des Achéens, malgré ce que pourrait laisser imaginer la scène dépeinte.").

[17] See especially Proclus's summary of the *Aethiopis*.

[18] *LIMC* Achilleus 854, 894. On the *Tabulae Iliacae*, see Valenzuela Montenegro 2004; Squire 2011; Petrain 2014 (199 for the scene under consideration here). See also *LIMC* 6.1:952, "Ulysse et la mort d'Achille," for further possible examples of Odysseus's involvement.

[19] Lehmann-Hartleben 1938, 97 and *LIMC* Achilleus 856. Both authors adduce Quintus of Smyrna to support the identification. At *Posthomerica* 3.308–319, Odysseus *does* suffer a wound, but he pays it no attention (ὃ δ᾽ ἕλκεος οὐκ ἀλέγιζεν, 3.311), and it is his opponent who falls to the ground before being killed.

[20] On this convention, see Avisseau-Broustet and Colonna 2017a, 210.

[21] I thank Guy Hedreen for drawing my attention to the importance of vertical juxtapositions between the necks and bodies of the pitchers.

[22] The tradition is as early as Homer (*Od.* 11.543–551) and a frequent subject in later literature.

[23] E.g., it goes unmentioned by Kossatz-Deissmann in her description at *LIMC* Achilleus 484.

[24] See *LIMC* Achilleus 478 (with bibliography), 479, 480, with Kossatz-Deissmann's commentary (1981, 121).

[25] *LIMC* Achilleus 537. For a catalogue of images that depict Phoenix's involvement at the arming scene, see *LIMC* Phoinix II, "Phoenix et les nouvelles armes d'Achille," 8.1 *Supplementum*, 986.

[26] Our image is not included in *LIMC* Phoinix II (8.1 *Supplementum*, 984–87).

[27] Cf. Dondin-Payre 2017, 66.

[28] Avisseau-Broustet and Colonna 2017a, 215 (epigraphic commentary by M. Dondin-Payre).

[29] See Dondin-Payre 2017, 67–68.

Works Cited

Avisseau-Broustet, M., and C. Colonna, eds. 2017a. *Le luxe dans l'antiquité: Trésors de la Bibliothèque nationale de France*. Gand: Éditions Snoeck.

———. 2017b. "Le trésor de Berthouville: Une découverte 'inattendue autant que merveilleuse.'" In *Le luxe dans l'antiquité: Trésors de la Bibliothèque nationale de France*, edited by M. Avisseau-Broustet and C. Colonna, 28–55. Gand: Éditions Snoeck.

Babelon, E. 1916. *Le trésor d'argenterie de Berthouville, près Bernay (Eure): Conservé au département des Médailles et antiques de la Bibliothèque nationale*. Paris: Librairie centrale des beaux-arts.

Bauer, A.A. 2019. "Itinerant Objects." *Annual Review of Anthropology* 48:335–52. DOI: 10.1146/annurev-anthro-102218-011111.

Canevaro, L.G. 2019. "Materiality and Classics." *JHS* 139:222–32. DOI: 10.1017/S0075426919000089.

Dondin-Payre, M. 2017. "Qu'apporte l'épigraphie à la connaissance du sanctuaire de Berthouville?" In *Le luxe dans l'antiquité: Trésors de la Bibliothèque nationale de France*, edited by M. Avisseau-Broustet and C. Colonna, 56–73. Gand: Éditions Snoeck.

Fauduet, I. 2017. "Le sanctuaire de Berthouville et son trésor dans le contexte de la Gaule romaine." In *Le luxe dans l'antiquité: Trésors de la Bibliothèque nationale de France*, edited by M. Avisseau-Broustet and C. Colonna, 74–87. Gand: Éditions Snoeck.

Kossatz-Deissmann, A. 1981. "Achilleus." *LIMC* 1.1:37–200.

———. 2009. "Achilleus." *LIMC Supplementum 2009* 1:2–15.

Lapatin, K., ed. 2014. *The Berthouville Silver Treasure and Roman Luxury*. Los Angeles: J. Paul Getty Museum.

Lehmann-Hartleben, K. 1938. "Two Roman Silver Jugs." *AJA* 42:82–105.

Nuber, H.U. 1974. "Silberfunde von Hildesheim und Berthouville." *BMusBrux* 46:23–30.

Petrain, D. 2014. *Homer in Stone: The Tabulae Iliacae in Their Roman Context*. Cambridge: Cambridge University Press.

Picard, C. 1948. "Sur les aiguières à sujets homériques du 'Trésor de Bernay' (Bibliothèque nationale)." *CRAI* 92:95–111. DOI: 10.3406/crai.1948.78225.

Sánchez, E., and S. Lansing Maish. 2014. "The Hidden Lives of Ancient Objects: Conserving the Berthouville Treasure and Four Missoria." In *The Berthouville Silver Treasure and Roman Luxury*, edited by K. Lapatin, 107–26. Los Angeles: J. Paul Getty Museum.

Squire, M. 2011. *The* Iliad *in a Nutshell: Visualizing Epic on the Tabulae Iliacae*. Oxford: Oxford University Press.

Valenzuela Montenegro, N. 2004. "Die *Tabulae Iliacae*: Mythos und Geschichte im Spiegel einer Gruppe frühkaiserzeitlicher Miniaturreliefs." Berlin: Dissertation.de.

The Many Lives of Chikaba's Jar

Sirio Canós-Donnay and Beatrijs G. de Groot

Abstract

Tucked away in a small cabinet in a convent in Salamanca (Spain) is a finely crafted little jar. Originally a filtered terra lemnia jar of Ottoman origin, it has since had a wide and diverse range of lives, from utilitarian object to Christian relic. In its life trajectory, it has woven together people, things, and historical processes across cultures, borders, and religions, from its origins in the island of Lemnos to its most famous owner, the 18th-century Afro-Hispanic nun and writer Teresa Chikaba. The jar's long and complex life trajectory illustrates and embodies a web of entangled lives, material processes, and global encounters. Through a combination of archival research and the reconstruction of the jar's origins, we have started to untangle these complex webs and traced some of the diverse past lives of this curious object and the stories it tells about the slave trade, relics, Islam, Christianity, court intrigues, politics, and racism in 18th-century Spain and beyond.[1]

Introduction: Entangled Itineraries and Global Histories

TUCKED AWAY IN A DISPLAY CASE IN CONVENTO DE LAS Dueñas in Salamanca (Spain), surrounded by a leather shoe and a wooden cup, is a cream-colored jar.[2] Approximately 25 cm high, the jar has a rounded body, straight neck, and one curved handle, at the base of which is a stamped seal (fig. 1). The body is covered with impressed decorations and remnants of gold leaf, and within the neck sits an ornately decorated filter. This unassuming jar connects a multiplicity of stories, from Ottoman diplomacy to the Atlantic slave trade, from Greek mythology to Victorian orientalism and Christian relics. This article attempts to unravel some of these stories, in particular those revolving around the life of the jar's last owner, the Afro-Hispanic nun Teresa Chikaba.[3] Using the jar as a central object in a web of historical connections, we explore how object biography/itinerary approaches can

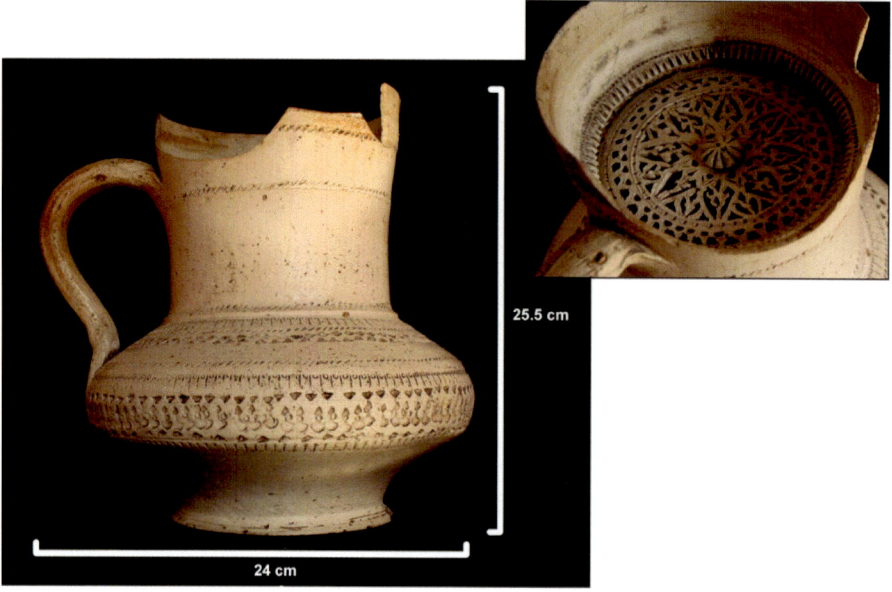

25.5 cm

24 cm

Fig. 1. Chikaba's jar and detail of the filter.

bring many past lives to the fore and allow us to explore the entangled trajectories of materials and people in the past.

Entangled in this web of connections is also our own research journey. We first came across the jar at the height of the COVID-19 pandemic in 2020. One of us (SCD) normally researches 13–19th-century West African states, so faced with the impossibility of traveling to West Africa, started to look instead at the presence of Africans in the Iberian Peninsula at the time. This led us to the story of Teresa Chikaba, and her tomb at the Convento de las Dueñas in Salamanca. A quick look at the Convent's *Tripadvisor* website revealed a very intriguing jar labeled "Chikaba's jar, African pottery." As soon as it was legal and feasible, we met and drove to Salamanca to study the jar in person. Tracing the entangled stories of Chikaba and the jar has since taken us (sometimes in person, sometimes virtually) to places as varied as Cambridge, Sicily, Ghana, Istanbul, Madrid, Venice, and Vienna, adding our own research journey to the jar's global web of interconnected histories.

Our research of the jar's trajectory combines object biography and itinerary approaches. Biographical approaches study the life of an object, as defined by the interactions and entanglements it has with people from its conception to its destruction.[4] In this sense, Chikaba's jar is still very much alive, as it is an object of continued interaction at the Convento de las Dueñas and, indeed, remotely, with us as we write this paper. Object itinerary approaches, on the other hand, enable us to analyze not only the jar's interactions, but also its prelife starting with the materiality of its geological deposits and the beliefs and practices that led to their excavation and use as raw material.[5] Combining historical and archaeological information from archives, monasteries, libraries, palaces, and museum depots, we seek to understand both Chikaba's journey and the jar's itinerary. This chapter is thus divided into two parts, summarizing our current understanding of Chikaba's journey and our preliminary insights from studying the jar.

Chikaba's Journey

Teresa Chikaba's life trajectory is as complex as it is fascinating.[6] Born in West Africa in the late 17th century, she was sold into slavery as a child and taken to Spain, where she would become the first known Afro-Hispanic writer and end her days as a highly regarded religious figure in a convent in Salamanca (see fig. 2). Most of the information we have about her life comes from her hagiography, written four years after her death by her last confessor, Juan Carlos Paniagua, which has been translated into English and insightfully annotated by B. Fra-Molinero and S.E. Houchins.[7] There are also shorter documents that provide clues about her life, including the will of the Marquise of Mancera (1703) that grants Chikaba her freedom, various records regarding her admission into the convent, a letter written by Chikaba herself, her funerary oration, and her obituary.[8] There is also a small amount of secondary literature on Chikaba and her life reflecting on the previously cited sources.[9]

Together, these documents draw a rough sketch of Chikaba's life, although many important gaps remain. According to Paniagua, Chikaba was born in Baja Mina del Oro in 1676. São Jorge da Mina (now Elmina) was a Portuguese settlement in what is currently Ghana, and the Gold Coast (*Costa del Oro* in Spanish) is how European traders referred to its surrounding area. Another element reinforcing the possible Ghanaian origin is her name, as *Tsika-ba* means "a small amount of gold" in Twi, a language spoken in central and southern Ghana.[10] Some authors have connected Chikaba to the kingdom of Ifsini (also known as Assini) in the current Ivory Coast. This is based on an episode in her hagiography in which a

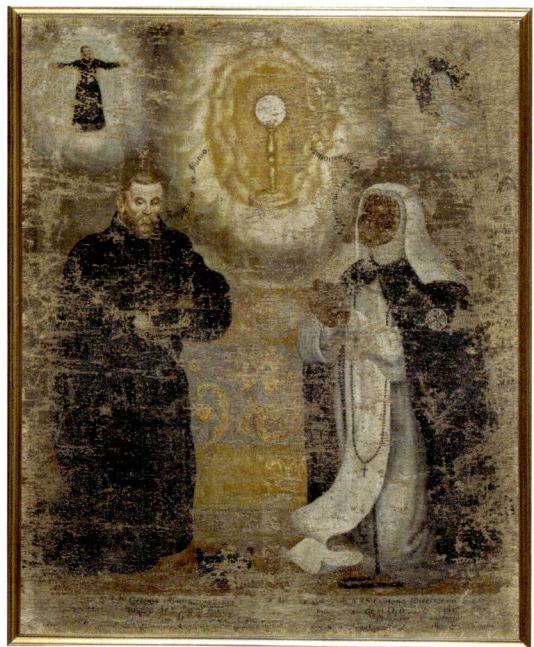

Fig. 2. Sister Teresa Chikaba and her confessor father Jerónimo Abarrategui, in a painting preserved at the Museo Provincial de Salamanca.

supposed uncle by the name of Juan Francisco visits her in Madrid after having spent some time in France at the court of Louis XIV. Some identify this character as Louis Aniaba, an Ifsini man that did spend some time in the French royal court, but we find the evidence inconclusive.[11]

Regardless of the specific origin, we know Chikaba was kidnapped/sold as a slave when she was around 10 years old, taken to São Tome and Principe, where she was baptized before being shipped again and taken to Sevilla. There, according to Paniagua, she was sold into a family that, recognizing her noble birth (she was said to be a princess) took her to King Carlos II in Madrid, who in turn gave her to the Marquises of Mancera.[12] Nevertheless, as Fra-Molinero and Houchins point out, the one surviving letter written by Chikaba denotes an Andalusian accent, suggesting she may have spent more time in Andalusia than Paniagua's version suggests.[13]

From her time in the Marquises' home in Madrid, we know only what Paniagua describes: that a governess was hired to teach her to write and read, that she shared lodgings with a Turkish enslaved girl, was beaten up on multiple occasions, received the above-mentioned visit of the supposed uncle, and started having religious visions. In 1703, the Marquise died, granting in her will Chikaba's freedom, as well as a dowry for entering a convent, and an annuity of 50 ducats for the rest of her life. Being accepted in a convent as a black woman in 18th-century Spain was no easy task, but eventually she was admitted as tertiary in the Dominican Monastery of the Penitence in Salamanca in 1704, where she lived until her death in 1748. During this time, she wrote poems and letters, and acquired a reputation as a healer and performer of miracles. She was initially buried in the same monastery where she had lived, but in 1810 her tomb had to be moved to a different location (the Monasterio de las Dueñas, also in Salamanca) to prevent looting by the Napoleonic troops. During this re-location, her shoes as well as some small bones were taken out to be used as relics.[14] Finally, in 1961, her tomb was moved from the monastery's cemetery to the current location in the cloisters.[15]

Her surviving belongings (the jar, the shoe, and a drinking cup with its case) were more recently placed in a display cabinet on the first floor of the cloisters to avoid further damage from devotees breaking off bits (see broken rim in fig. 1) to take them home for healing purposes, as had been happening until then.[16] To this day, devotion for Chikaba continues to be strong in Salamanca, and multiple faith groups are working to promote her canonization. Her fame has also crossed the ocean, becoming a well-known figure among black Catholics across the world, as shown by her depiction in a stained glass window at St. Dominic Chapel in Providence College (US).

The Pot's Journey

Following our visit to the convent in June 2021, our first task was to identify the provenance and nature of the jar. The filter and stamped seal clearly placed it in the realm of Islamic ceramics, but the precise origin and type were unclear, with no matches in Spanish pottery repertoires at the time. Filtered water jars were produced in Iran and Egypt since the 8th century, with well-known examples deriving from Fustat, Egypt's capital during the Umayyad and Abbasid caliphates.[17] However, the Fustat jars are significantly coarser, wheel-made, and unburnished, and do not match Chikaba's jar in either style or decoration. After several months of unproductive searches and a long string of negative replies from specialists unable to identify it, we finally found a promising match: a jar at the Ashmolean Museum in Oxford that presented very similar decoration, filter, technological characteristics, and stamp location. Along with this jar was a single bibliographic reference: J. Raby's 1995 paper "Terra Lemnia and the Potteries of the Golden Horn," which would completely change the direction of our research. Chikaba's jar was none other than a *terra lemnia*: a type of Ottoman ceramics made with clays from the Greek island of Lemnos in a revival of a classical ritual described by Galen. This clay was believed to have antipoison properties and was taken to Istanbul to be sold in stamped *pastilles* and shaped into beautiful filtered water jars to be used by the sultan and his viziers, as well as diplomatic gifts.

The Clay: Lemnos

Clay from the island of Lemnos has been valued since classical times, in particular for its medicinal properties. Pliny (*Naturalis Historia* 35.33; 29.104; 18.88) and Galen (*Opera Omnia* 12.169–73) discuss its use as a treatment for snakebites and poisoning, as well as viral infections like the plague. Interestingly, at this point there are no records of the clay being turned into pots, only consumed. Galen details how the extraction of the clay could only happen once a year and was marked by elaborate rituals, in which a priestess prepared the ground for excavation, and the obtained clay would then be washed and marked with a stamp. Hence how the clay gained its name *terra sigillata* (sealed earth), though we follow Raby in referring to it as *terra lemnia* to avoid confusion with the Roman ware.[18]

The mining of *terra lemnia* appears to have then gradually faded over the centuries, as suggested by the lack of mentions in the accounts of travelers to the island and historians alike.[19] The texts singing its praises, however, were preserved (see fig. 3), and eventually reached the Ottoman Sultan Mehmed the Conqueror, who after claiming Lemnos back from the Venetians in 1479, sent various delegations to locate the source of the clay and resume its mining.[20] One direct witness to this Ottoman revival of *terra lemnia* was 16th-century traveler and diplomat Pierre Belon, who visited the island and described how clay was excavated yearly on August 6 (the same day as in classical times) for six hours only, as part of an elaborate ceremony that combined orthodox Christian elements with pre-Christian practices. The clay was then processed and stamped, with the majority being dispatched directly to Istanbul, while in Lemnos capital punishment was reserved to

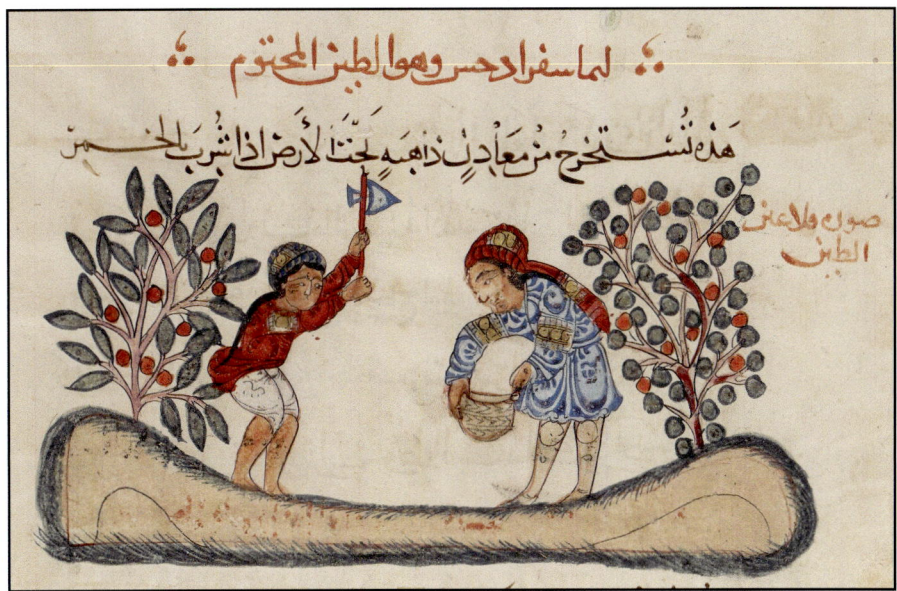

انه هوالطبز المحتوم ٠٠ لما سفرا دحسر وهوالطبز المحتوم ٠٠
هذا نشتخرج من معادن ذاهبه حت الأرض إذا اشرب بالخمر
صور ولاعن الطبز

Ottoman mining in the island appears to have continued until the late 19th century.[22]

Once in Istanbul, the earth was put to two uses: sealed *pastilles* to be consumed for their medicinal properties and clay for special pots and vessels. An element that the Ottomans particularly valued in *terra lemnia* was its supposed antipoison properties, particularly the Greek physician Discorides claimed that if dissolved in wine, *terra lemnia* acts as an antidote to poison, which had been preserved in copies of classical texts (see fig. 3). In fact, it is reported that the Ottoman sultan himself would grate a small portion of *terra lemnia* over his daily food to avoid poisoning.[23] The second and new use of the clay, as a material for pottery-making, was also inspired by its supposed medical properties. Henry Tozer, who traveled to Lemnos in 1889 to record the tradition, describes how the Ottomans believed that ceramics made from the clay could neutralize the effects of any poison put inside them.[24]

Did clay from Lemnos genuinely have the medical properties classical and Ottoman authors attributed to it? Over the past decades several studies have tried to answer this question through geochemical and mineralogical methods.[25] Results have been mixed: *pastilles* from a Basel collection were demonstrated to have a significant antibacterial effect against

Fig. 3. 1224 C.E. Iraqi copy of the Greek physician Discorides's De materia medica, describing the antipoison properties of terra lemnia, illustrated by two men excavating clay in Lemnos (adapted from, Freer Gallery of Art and Atil 1975, 57).

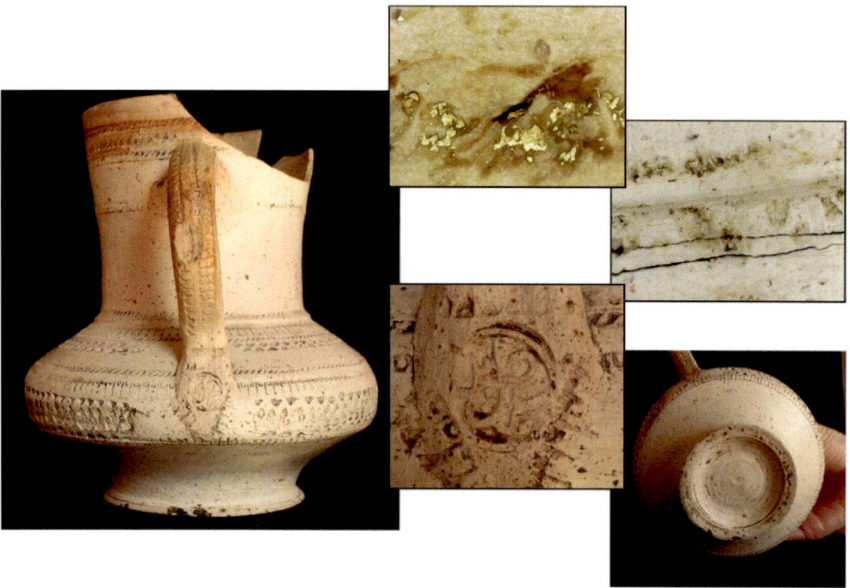

Fig. 4. Chikaba's jar with images of details discussed in the text. From top to bottom; gold leaf decoration; horizontal cracks along neck/ filter join, the stamp, rilling on base.

Staphylococcus aureus, a common Gram-positive pathogen, while unprocessed clays from the Lemnos did not.[26]

The Manufacturing Process in Istanbul

While there are reports of some *terra lemnia* jars being produced in Lemnos itself, the vast majority were manufactured in Istanbul, more specifically in the earthenware potters quarter located in the Golden Horn.[27] This is almost certainly the case of Chikaba's jar, given its typological similarities with Iznik pottery.[28] Chikaba's jar is 24 cm wide and 25.5 cm high with a cylindrical neck, globular body, ring-base, and one loop-handle connecting the neck and body. The jar is cream colored with a band of leaf gold located at the rim, which has largely disappeared save for a few traces (fig. 4). It is decorated with triangular, vertical, rounded, and hour-glass shaped impressions covering the belly, rim, and handle, and it has an elaborately decorated filter with a central button located some 7.5 cm below the top of the rim.

The jar is at least partially made on a potter's wheel, although rilling (horizontal lines on the vessel surface which are traces of the use of a potter's wheel) and other traces are invisible due to the careful burnishing of the vessel surface, with horizontal burnishing marks on the body and diagonal and vertical marks of the neck. Rilling is visible at the bottom of the ring base, indicating that the pot was finished upside down on the wheel when leather-hard. Ottoman potters used kick wheels for ceramic production, composed of a lower wheel mounted to a pivot and wheel-head at the top;[29] the lower wheel would act as a fly-wheel allowing the top wheel to reach significant rotational speed. The neck was probably slab-built and placed on the jar after the application of the filter. The vertical burnishing marks overlap the area where the rim and body are attached. Small stress cracks are visible at the base of the neck where the filter is situated, relating to differences in the drying times of the main body and neck. The fabric is cream colored with small brownish specks suggesting the clay was tempered.

Like all *terra lemnia* vessels, Chikaba's jar has a stamped seal at the base of the handle containing two words (see fig. 4). The most common inscription in *terra lemnia* jars is *tin-i-mahtun* (lit. "stamped earth"), but the style in which it is written varies substantially (see fig. 5). Another common option are stamps that identify the potter, such as *amal* (work of) + potter's name.[30] The seal in Chikaba's jar is mostly illegible, as the impression is shallow and the characters are not well-defined, but it seems clear that it does not say either *amal* + name or *tin-i-mahtun*. The Dominican nuns believe the stamp reads "Halim made me" or "Halim made it," but this does not fit either with the characters that are legible.[31] The two most probable readings for the seal are *Sābir 'Azīz* (the name of the potter or first owner) or *Sābiru 'Azīzun* ("he who is patient is mighty," a maxim), but the lack of definition in the impression makes it difficult to ascertain in the absence of a better impressed seal by the same maker.[32]

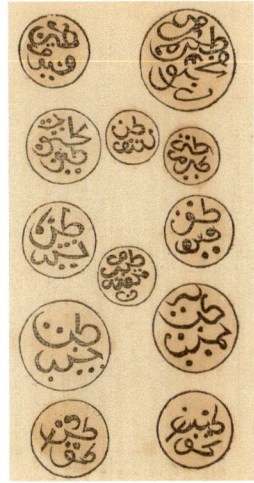

Fig. 5. Range of terra lemnia seals documented by P. Belon in 1554 (Belon 1554, 24).

From Istanbul to the World

In order to understand how Chikaba became the owner of such a unique and prestigious item, it is necessary to understand how *terra lemnia* jars traveled outside of Istanbul. We know from Ottoman records that while production of *terra lemnia* vessels was quite substantial, particularly in the 17th century, there was also significant variation in clay qualities and vessel types. The most prestigious jars (like that of Chikaba) were used as presents for the sultan and his viziers and exported as diplomatic gifts.[33] The demand for *terra lemnia* gradually spread across Europe following its Ottoman revival, and by the late 16th century both *pastilles* and vessels had become highly valued in courts and cabinets of curiosities across the continent.[34] For example, Belon confirms that ambassadors to Turkey often returned home with pieces of *terra lemnia*.[35]

While mentions of *terra lemnia pastilles* are relatively common, those of vessels are significantly scarcer. The earliest record of a *terra lemnia* vessel in a non-Turkish collection comes from the *Wunderkammer* of Rudolph II (1552–1612). The *Wunderkammer's* inventory, drawn up between 1607 and 1611, lists eight Ottoman vessels under the heading "*Terrae Sigillatae Geschirrlein, Türkisch,*" three of which are still preserved in the Kunsthistorisches Museum in Vienna (see table 1).[36] Another documented example consists of two jars, currently in the Biblioteca Ambrosiana in Milan, but originally from the collection of Manfredo Settala (1600–1680), Milanese cleric and scientist whose cabinet of curiosities was one of the most extensive in Italy.[37] The Palazzo Abatellis in Palermo, sometimes described as the "Sicilian Wunderkammer," also has at least seven *terra lemnia* jars (see table 1).[38]

The multiple examples in British museums, on the other hand, appear to be mostly late-19th–early 20th-century acquisitions, often involving interconnected individuals. The earliest set of (12) jars was acquired in 1875 by the Victoria & Albert Museum from George Morris, the British Consul in Sicily, who had previously been engaged in collecting objects for the British Museum in Asia Minor. This purchase is said to have been recommended by A.W. Franks of the British Museum and supervised by C.D.E. Fortnum.[39] Fortnum is also listed as the supplier of the *terra lemnia* jar acquired by the Ashmolean in 1888;[40] while Franks supplied another jar for the British Museum in 1894. The British Museum's collection of *terra lemnia* jars was complemented by further acquisitions in 1878 (J. Henderson, one jar), 1909 (E. Dillon, six jars), and 1974 (anonymous, three jars). The Fitzwilliam's 10 jars, on the other hand, are the result of two donations, one by J.W.L. Glaisher in 1928 (one) and another by Sir Austin Harris in 1938 (nine). While the specific profile of each donor varied, all of them were wealthy art collectors, sometimes with connections to Turkey or Sicily.[41]

Conclusion: Chikaba, the World, and a Small Pot

In this study, we have traced back three sets of itineraries (our research path, Chikaba's life, and the jar's trajectory) and explored the entangled lives, material processes, and global

Table 1. List of *terra lemnia* jars in European and private collections.

Museum/ Collection	Location	Number of jars	Catalogue/Auction references	Bibliography
British Museum	London, UK	11	1878,1230.354.a; 1894,0614.4; 1909,0616.1; 1909,0616.2; 1909,0616.3; 1909,0616.4; 1909,0616.5; 1909,0616.6; OA+.705;OA+.706; OA+.707	-Hobson 1932 -Raby 1995 -Rogers 1983
Victoria & Albert Museum	London, UK	12	918:1, 2-1875; 919-1875; 920-1875; 922-1875; 921-1875; 923-1875; 924-1875; 925-1875; 926:1, 2-1875; 927-1875; 928-1875; 929-1875	-Raby 1995
Fitzwilliam Museum	Cambridge, UK	10	OC.1754-1928; OC.103-1938; OC.104-1938; OC.105 & A-1938; OC.106-1938; OC.107-1938; OC.108-1938; OC.109-1938; OC.110-1938; OC.111-1938	
Private Collection	Sold at Sotheby's in 2016	1	Arts of the Islamic World Auction, 19 Oct 2016, Lot 289.	
Ashmolean Museum	Oxford, UK	1	EAX.1787	
Kunsthistorisches Museum	Vienna, Austria	At least 3	KK 3159; KK 3170; KK 3128	
Biblioteca Ambrosiana	Milan, Italy	At least 2		-Aimi et al. 1984
Galleria Regionale della Sicilia	Palermo, Italy	At least 7	6268; 6276; 6281; 6285; 6297; 6301; 6307	-Abbate 2001 -Curatola 1993
Private Collection	Sold at Christie's in 1994	1	26.04.1994, Lot 390	-Abbate 2001

encounters that define them. As I. Kopytoff has pointed out, societies construct objects as they construct people; this means humans can be often commoditized while objects can also be singularized.[42] Thus, human and object biographies, although completely different in terms of agency, often present remarkably similar narrative structures. In the case of Chikaba and her jar, their intersecting biographies stress the movement of objects and people across time and space and through different types of social status, from commodities (enslaved person, trade item) to prestigious entities (writer and revered nun, diplomatic gift), as well as medical specialists (healer, antipoison jug) and loci of worship (potential saint, relic). Approaching these biographies as combined journeys allows us to understand the entangled relations between people and things and the wider significance of both.

The journeys described here are still ongoing: Chikaba is currently in the process of being canonized, the jar may soon be restored, and our research journey still has important gaps to fill. One key element yet to be answered is how the pot came to be in Chikaba's possession: Was it through the friendship with the Turkish girl in the Marquis's house? If so, who was this girl and how did such a prestigious object fall into her hands? Or was it perhaps a gift earned through Chikaba's passage through the Spanish royal court? But why would the king of Spain give away what was possibly the only such object in his collection to a passing enslaved servant?[43] Could this be a gift of the Marquise, whose will shows she genuinely cared about Chikaba (although not enough to free her before her death)? At the moment we can only speculate but we hope future research will cast further light on these matters.

Other questions remain about the origin of the jar itself. Could it be a forgery or are we dealing with a jar from proper Lemnian clay? What more can be learned about the scale and context of production of these jars, and the artists behind their elaborate designs? Comparative research and geochemical analyses could also provide further lines of evidence for the scale and context of their production, perhaps allowing us to link jars made by the same crafts producers.

For now, the exploration of the biographies of both Chikaba and her jar has already provided important insights: we have an Ottoman jar made with clay mined following a Christian Orthodox ritual with pagan origins, that becomes a Catholic relic through its association with a West African nun. The combined journeys of Chikaba and her jar take us from classical Greece to 21st century Spain, from slave traders in the Gulf of Guinea to the Ottoman royal court. They tell us stories of trade and adaptation, of prejudice and friendship, of people treated like things and things that represent people. Most importantly, they shine a bright light on the global web of historical connections that a single object can weave throughout its life.

Notes

[1] We want to express our gratitude to Sor M. Eugenia Maeso and the rest of the Dominican congregation for allowing us to study and record the jar in the Convento de las Dueñas. We would also like to thank J. Raby, V. Apaydin, P. Rainer, R. Blench, and B. Fra-Molinero for taking the time to reply to our queries with such helpful comments. Finally, this research was supported by Leverhulme-Trust Early Career Fellowship (Grant nr: ECF-2019-081, BdG), and a Marie Skłodowska-Curie Fellowship (MSCA-IF-EF-ST/0542-844159, SCD), as well as logistical support from INCIP-IT-CSIC.

[2] The leather shoe was extracted from Chikaba's coffin when her body was moved to the current monastery in 1810. The small wooden cup comes with a leather holder and lid with a label reading "baso por donde vebió el Niño Jesús [sic]" ("glass from which Baby Jesus drank," author translation). Its origin and connection to Chikaba are unclear.

[3] As we shall explain later, Chikaba was probably never accepted as a full nun, but rather as a "tertiary," a lay member of the congregation. Nevertheless, she wore the habit, lived in the convent, and for all intents and purposes lived like the rest of the sisters in the congregation, albeit in a more subaltern position.

[4] Kopytoff 1986; Gosden and Marshall 1999; Joy 2009.

[5] Joyce and Gillespie 2015.

[6] Also sometimes known as Teresa Juliana de Santo Domingo.

[7] A hagiography (lit. "holy writing") is a biography of a saint or a highly regarded religious leader. In the case of Chikaba it was written by her last confessor with the goal of initiating Chikaba's canonization process. Paniagua 1752. Fra-Molinero and Houchins 2018.

[8] Her will: *Testamento de Doña Juliana Teresa de Portocarreño, Marquesa de Manciora* (Archivo Histórico de Protocolos Notariales, Madrid. 10 April 1703. Libro 13.977, fol. 135v). A copy and transcription can be found in Fra-Molinero and Houchins (2018, 277). Her admission to convent: the *Acta de Profesión* (preserved at the Archivo Histórico del Monasterio de las Madres Dominicas Dueñas de Salamanca; Sección Convento de la Penitencia) and the *Carta de Pago* (preserved at the Archivo Histórico Provincial de Salamanca,

Oficio 7, escribano Juan Antonio de Paz, Sección de Protocolos Notariales; 19 abril 1704; Protocolo 3931, fols. 613r–615v). Both documents are also reproduced, transcribed and translated in Fra-Molinero and Houchins 2018, appendix 1 and 2. A photograph of her letter is included in Maeso (1985, 31), and a transcription can be read in Fra-Molinero and Houchins (2018, 41). Her funerary oration: Paniagua 1749. Her obituary: *Acta Capituli Provincialis provinciae Hispaniae Ordinis Praedicatorum, celebrati in conventu Sancti Ildephonsi Regali Taurensi Die 27 Aprilis, anni Domini 1749* (Madrid, 1749). A transcription can be found in appendix 3 of Fra-Molinero and Houchins 2018.

[9] Martín-Casares 2000; Maeso 2004; Ferrús Antón 2008; Melián 2012; Benoist 2015; Fra-Molinero and Houchins 2018; Philips 2020.

[10] Christaller 1933.

[11] E.g., Melián 2012, 568.

[12] Paniagua 1752, 20–23.

[13] Fra-Molinero and Houchins 2018, 41.

[14] *Acta del traslado de los restos de Sor Teresa del Convento de la Penitencia al de Dominicas Dueñas*, reproduced in Maeso 1985, 24.

[15] Maeso 1985, 15.

[16] M. Eugenia Maeso, pers. comm.

[17] Scanlon 1970; Joel and Peli 2006.

[18] Raby 1995, 307.

[19] Raby 1995, 322.

[20] The story of the rediscovery is narrated in detail by the Armenian doctor Amirtovlat of Amasya, a member of the sultan's entourage in his 1482 book *Useless to the Ignorant*, a translation of the relevant fragments can be read in Raby 1995, 325.

[21] Belon 1554, 25; Raby 1995, 315.

[22] Raby 1995, 321.

[23] Belon 1554, 23–24; Crusius 1584, 508; Raby 1995, 315–6.

[24] Tozer 1890, 264.

[25] E.g., Hall and Photos-Jones 2008; Photos-Jones et al. 2017.

[26] For the Basel collection, see Photos-Jones et al. 2017. For unprocessed clay, see Hall and Photos-Jones 2008.

[27] For Lemnos, see, e.g., Tozer 1890, 265. For Istanbul, see Kütükoğlu 1983; Raby 1995, 330.

[28] E.g., Atasoy and Raby 1989.

[29] Atasoy and Raby 1989.

[30] See, e.g., *amalfalak ali hassan* inscription featured in a *terra lemnia* jar very similar to Chikaba's sold in Sotheby's in 2016 (see table 1).

[31] Maeso 1985, 16.

[32] We would like to thank J. Raby and V. Apaydin for their generosity and assistance with the interpretation of the inscription.

[33] Raby 1995, 330.

[34] Raby 1995, 318.

[35] Belon 1554, 23.

[36] P. Reiner, pers. comm.

[37] For Biblioteca Ambrosiana, see Aimi et al. 1984. For Settala, see Tavernari 1976.

[38] Abbate 2001.

[39] Victoria & Albert Museum 2009.

[40] Ashmolean Museum 2013.

[41] Sir Austin Harris's younger brother Clement fought in the 1897 Greco-Turkish war and died in a hospital there (Cadbury Research Library 2023), J. Henderson donated a substantial quantity of Turkish ceramics to the British Museum (Jenyns 1953, 104).

[42] Kopytoff 1986.

[43] The Spanish royal house object inventory (Catálogo GOYA, Patrimonio Nacional) does not currently include any *terra lemnia* jars. While it cannot be ruled out that such objects may have been owned by the royal family before (particularly given the change in royal houses in 1700), they were clearly not abundant.

Works Cited

Abbate, V. 2001. *Wunderkammer siciliana: Alle origini del museo perduto*. Naples: Electa Napoli.

Aimi, A., V. De Michele, and A. Morandotti. 1984. *Septalianum musæum: Una collezione scientifica nella Milano del Seicento*. Firenze: Giunti Marzocco.

Ashmolean Museum. 2013. *Jug with Rosette Filter inside the Neck*. http://jameelcentre.ashmolean.org/collection/8/per_page/25/offset/0/sort_by/material/object/10953.

Atasoy, N., and J. Raby. 1989. *Iznik: The Pottery of Ottoman Turkey*. Edited by Y. Petsopoulos. London: Thames & Hudson.

Belon, P. 1554. *Les Observations de plusieurs singularitez et choses mémorables trouvées en Grèce, Asie, Judée, Égypte, Arabie et autres pays estranges, rédigées en trois livres*. Paris: Guillaume Cauellat.

Benoist, V. 2015. "La doble identidad de sor Chicaba/Teresa." In *Actas Del III Congreso Ibero-Africano de Hispanistas*, edited by N. Achiri, Á. Baraibar, and F.K.E. Schmelzer, 147–56. Pamplona: Universidad de Navarra.

Cadbury Research Library. 2023. *European Travel Journal of Walter Burton Harris [1882]*. https://calmview.bham.ac.uk/Record.aspx?src=Catalog&id=XMS161.

Christaller, J.G. 1933. *Dictionary of the Asante and Fante Language Called Tshi (Twi)*. 2nd ed. Basel: Basel Evangelical Missionary Society.

Crusius, M. 1584. *Turcograecia Libri Octo*. Basile: Henricpetrus Ostein.

Curatolla, G. 1993. *Eredità dell'Islam: Arte Islamica in Italia*. Venice: Silvana Editoriale.

Ferrús Antón, B. 2008. "Sor Teresa Juliana de Santo Domingo, 'Chicaba' o escribir en la piel del otro." *Cuadernos Dieciochistas* 9:181–92.

Fra-Molinero, B., and S.E. Houchins. 2018. *Black Bride of Christ: Chicaba, an African Nun in Eighteenth-Century Spain.* Nashville: Vanderbilt University Press.

Freer Gallery of Art and E. Atil. 1975. *Art of the Arab World.* Washington: Smithsonian Institution.

Gosden, C., and Y. Marshall. 1999. "The Cultural Biography of Objects." *WorldArch* 312:169–78. DOI: 10.1080/00438243.1999.9980439.

Hall, A.J., and E. Photos-Jones. 2008. "Accessing Past Beliefs and Practices: The Case of Lemnian Earth." *Archaeometry* 50:1034–49. DOI: 10.1111/j.1475-4754.2007.00377.x.

Hobson, R.L. 1932. *A Guide to the Islamic Pottery of the Near East.* London: British Museum.

Jenyns, S. 1953. "The Franks Collection of Oriental Antiquities." *The British Museum Quarterly* 18:103–6. DOI: 10.2307/4422450.

Joel, G., and A. Peli. 2006. *Suse, terres cuites islamiques.* Paris: Musée du Louvre.

Joy, J. 2009. "Reinvigorating Object Biography: Reproducing the Drama of Object Lives." *WorldArch* 41:540–56. DOI: 10.1080/00438240903345530.

Joyce, R.A., and S.D. Gillespie, eds. 2015. *Things in Motion: Object Itineraries in Anthropological Practice.* Santa Fe: SAR Press.

Kopytoff, I. 1986. "The Cultural Biography of Things: Commoditization as Process." In *The Social Life of Things: Commodities in Cultural Perspective,* edited by A. Appadurai, 64–91. Cambridge: Cambridge University Press. DOI: 10.1017/CBO9780511819582.004.

Kütükoğlu, M.S. 1983. *Osmanlılarda narh müessesesi ve 1640 tarihli narh defteri.* Istanbul: Enderun Kitabevi.

Maeso, M.E. 1985. *Tshikaba, la princesa negra.* Salamanca: Dominicas Dueñas.

———. 2004. *Sor Teresa Chikaba: Princesa, esclava y monja.* Salamanca: Editorial San Esteban.

Martín-Casares, A. 2000. "Cristianos, musulmanes y animistas en Granada: identidades religiosas y sincretismo cultural." In *Negros, mulatos y zambaigos: Derroteros africanos en los mundos ibéricos,* edited by B. Ares Queija and A. Stella, 207–21. Paris: Centre National de la Recherche Scientifique.

Melián, E.M. 2012. "Chikaba, la primera monja negra en el sistema esclavista finisecular español del siglo XVII." *Hispania sacra* 64, no. 130:565–81. DOI: 10.3989/hs.2012.017.

Paniagua, J.C.M. 1749. *Oracion funebre en las exequias de la Madre Sor Teresa Juliana de Santo Domingo, de feliz memoria, celebradas en el dia nueve de enero en el Convento de Religiosas Dominicas, vulgo de la Penitencia.* Salamanca.

————. 1752. *Compendio de la vida exemplar de la Venerable Madre Sor Teresa Juliana de Sto. Domingo, tercera professa en el Convento de Santa Maria Magdalena, vulgo de la Penitencia, Orden de Santo Domingo de la Ciudad de Salamanca.* Salamanca.

Phillips, B.M. 2020. "Docile Bodies and the Walls of Female Confinement Past and Present: A Biopolitical Look at Orange Is the New Black and Chicaba." In *Confined Women: The Walls of Female Space in Early Modern Spain*, edited by B.M. Phillips and E. Colbert Cairns, 209–25. Minneapolis: Hispanic Issues Online. https://conservancy.umn.edu/bitstream/handle/11299/212983/hiol_25_11_phillips.pdf?sequence=1&isAllowed=y.

Photos-Jones, E., C. Edwards, F. Häner, L. Lawton, C. Keane, A. Leanord, and V. Perdikatsis. 2017. "Archaeological Medicinal Earths as Antibacterial Agents: The Case of the Basel Lemnian *sphragides*." *Geological Society, London, Special Publications* 452:141–53. DOI: 10.1144/SP452.6.

Raby, J. 1995. "Terra Lemnia and the Potteries of the Golden Horn: An Antique Revival under Ottoman Auspices." *Byzantische Forschungen* 21:305–42.

Rogers, J.M. 1983. *Islamic Art and Design: 1500–1700.* London: British Museum.

Scanlon, G.T. 1970. "Fāṭimid Filters: Archaeology and Olmer's Typology." *Annales Islamogiques* 9:37–64.

Tavernari, C. 1976. Manfredo Settala, collezionista e scienziato milanese del'600. *Annali dell'Istituto e Museo di storia della scienza di Firenze* 1:43–61. DOI: 10.1163/221058776X00057.

Tozer, H. F. 1890. *The Islands of the Aegean.* Oxford: Clarendon Press.

Victoria & Albert Museum. 2009. *Cup and Cover, ca. 1800–1875.* https://collections.vam.ac.uk/item/O225550/cup-and-cover-unknown/.

Biographical Perspectives on the Materiality of a Diaspora: Teapots of Greek-Australian Migrants from Kythera

Christina Marini and Lita Tzortzopoulou-Gregory

Abstract

During the interwar period and the decades following the end of WWII, the population of Kythera—a small island in southwestern Greece—saw a rapid decrease and restructuring through mass migration to Australia. Building on the growing cross-disciplinary interest on the materiality of migration and modern diasporas, this study employs object biography or rather its analytical descendant, object itinerary, to explore the intersection of materiality and this case of transnational mobility.

The material focus of the chapter is a group oʀ three electroplated teapots, currently owned by individuals residing on Kythera. The teapots were originally used in the so-called Greek cafés: iconic establishments run by Kytherian and other Greek migrants in Australia, which are central when approaching the materiality of the Greek migrant communities. The itineraries of the teapots demonstrate how individual migratory experiences shaped the meanings, emotions, and relational connections associated with the objects. Framing the analysis within the object biographical discourse offers a closer look into how objects create tangible and performative links to people, places, and experiences, become entangled with aspects of collective identification and heritage, and capture the inbetweenness of the diasporic experience.[1]

Introduction

The intersection of materiality and the various modes of human mobility is a rapidly growing field across social sciences. Albeit the theme is by no means new to archaeology, the material turn and posthumanist thinking have radically reshaped how human–object interactions are problematized and have set their pertinence to migration research on new theoretical and methodological grounds. The present study, building on the object-biographical discourse, focuses on a group of three at first glance inconspicuous-looking 20th-century electroplated teapots, recorded on the island of Kythera, in southwestern Greece, in 2022. The objects followed long and complex itineraries—to use the ontologically updated analytical construct—from commodities, and parts of business assemblages, to symbolically and emotionally charged memorabilia intersecting with the lives of their owners and the experiences of the Greek-Australian diasporic communities.

The teapots are owned by individuals interviewed on Kythera, as part of the Finds Stories project—an interdisciplinary research that involves archaeologists, anthropologists, museologists, educators, and creative artists, and investigates cases of intra-Balkan mobility, from antiquity to today through object and people biographies. The factors that warranted the selection of the teapots, fully addressed below, boil down to their close association with the Greek café, a business type that would become synonymous to Greek entrepreneurship in Australia. Retracing their itineraries offers the opportunity to observe the entanglement of these material artifacts with matters of self- and collective identification, memory, and heritage. Weaving together multilayered narratives, as the objects entered and exited people's lives, and moved across time and geopolitical borders, we aim to explore how the meanings and values assigned to the teapots were shaped by, but also themselves informed the identities of their owners within a specific transnational context. The discussion particularly adopts a perspective that stems from diaspora studies, as it captures in the most representative way the notion of hybridity and the complexity of connections between premigration pasts and the migratory presents, which extend beyond conceptualizations of nationality or ethnicity.

Kythera and Overseas Migration

As to why Kythera proves an appropriate place to start when pursuing the interplay of materiality and migration in our case study, the answer lies exactly on the fact that mass-migratory flows have more than anything else defined modern-day realities on the island. Kythera, despite its strategic location, partway between the Greek mainland and Crete (fig. 1), situated across diachronically frequented routes connecting the western and eastern Mediterranean, has always held a peripheral position to major political and economic decision-

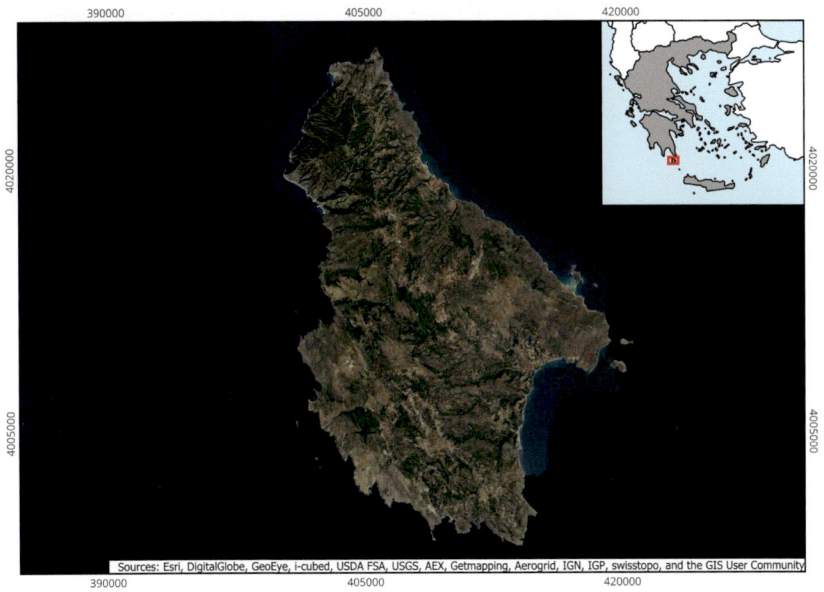

making. Over the past three centuries, the island changed hands between different empires and spheres of economic and political control, from Ottoman, Venetian, and French rule, to becoming part of a British protectorate until its eventual cession to modern Greece in 1864.[2] Worldwide changes, paired with the scarcity of natural resources on the island and the overall low degree of industrialization of insular Greek economies, triggered large-scale movements of Kytherians away from the island in the course of the 20th century.

Fig. 1. Map of Kythera (by S. Biernath).

As opposed to the 19th century Kytherian migration, oriented toward flourishing commercial centers of the Ottoman Empire, such as Istanbul, Izmir in Asia Minor, and Alexandria in Egypt, the 20th century migratory patterns, were partly directed toward the Greek capital but most predominantly overseas.[3] Between the 1890s and the 1920s Kytherians migrated primarily toward the United States and to a lesser degree Australia, while a much stronger second migratory wave during the interwar and the post-WWII era, was directed almost exclusively toward Australia.[4] These trajectories reflect Greek migratory flows as a whole, but Kythera stands out because of the sheer volume and extent of the population movement toward Australia.[5] It is estimated that there are now more than 50,000 people of Kytherian descent in Sydney alone, while the island at present has a population of around

3,500, of which a significant number is that of recently arrived immigrants mostly from Albania and eastern Europe, as well as a sizeable number of European, United Kingdom, and United States expats. The Kytherian diasporic community in Australia has for generations nurtured a lasting connection with the island, not only by means of revenues, financial investment, and tourism, but also by fueling a strand of return migration and by engaging in cultural ventures both in Australia and on Kythera.

It is individuals of Kytherian-Australian descent that the teapots, whose itineraries this chapter examines, belong to and their stories relate to their individual and diasporic experiences. The narratives associated with the objects, as reconstructed from material documentation and oral testimonies, and presented below, aim to demonstrate the complex reciprocal interactions between the vessels and their owners, informed by the places and social contexts they circulated in. The discussion that follows explores the ever-progressing transformation of the vessels from commodities to symbolic objects resignified by their transnational connections.

Migration, Materiality, and Our Methodology

The connection of material artifacts and consumption patterns with the migratory experience lies in the capacity of objects to function as physical and performative links to places, people, memories, and feelings, creating a sense of continuity between the "here" and "there." Their significance for exploring voluntary or forced migration, as well as processes of diasporization is increasingly acknowledged.[6] Research has particularly focused on the possessions of first-generation migrants, or on domestic assemblages, in their capacity to create a sense of belonging and to encompass memories, relationships, and family dynamics.[7] Interest in public and communal contexts is, on the other hand, much more limited.[8] The itineraries of objects—in our case the teapots—that were intertwined with the business ventures of Greek-Australian migrants, thus, offer a fresh insight into how material practices outside the domestic sphere are equally crucial in the articulation of a shared imagery, and the mediation of imagined connections to a common tradition or background within a specific diasporic group.

Contemporary archaeology itself has contributed in diverse ways to migration and diaspora studies, offering methodological means for investigating matters of materiality.[9] What the biographical approach, advocated in this chapter, adds to the discourse is the possibility of examining the complex entanglements of material artifacts and their multidirectional relational connections from a closeup and individualized scope, giving a nuanced perspective into personal migratory experiences. We particularly adopt the updated concept of object itinerary, due to the emphasis it places on movement—literally as well as figuratively—across time, space, and different networks of relationships.[10] Understanding the objects as being in a constant process of becoming, deeply entangled with the lives of the people they interact with and the social contexts they inhabit, demonstrates how people and things can only be understood in relationships with each other that are situationally defined.[11] In this way, itineraries prove particularly relevant to analyzing diasporic communities, since connections to "home" have been shown to be dynamic and ever-transforming. Much like the itineraries of the objects, the diasporic communities are in an ever-progressing state of redefining themselves, similar to other imagined communities.[12] The individual itineraries of the objects can thus illustrate how meanings and associations of material elements shift, contributing to the construction of shared—albeit not uniformly perceived—narratives.

Guided by the above theoretical considerations, our sampling methodology was therefore aimed at reconstructing itineraries of objects identified as representative of individual transnational experiences. In the course of our fieldwork campaign, which was more broadly focused on contemporary migrants and return migrants on Kythera, we had the opportunity to interview 14 individuals, currently residing on the island on a permanent or seasonal basis. The volunteers, aged between 45 and 90 years old, with a wide range of levels of education and occupations, participated by supplying objects they felt a strong attachment to, in relation to their personal or family migratory journey, and by consenting to an accompanying interview process. Nine of the interviewed individuals and 30 of the 45 recorded objects that resulted from this campaign were associated with the migratory movements to and from Australia.

The documentation process, besides the initial cataloguing of formal characteristics, aimed to identify and outline biographical parameters—in other words knots in the itineraries of the objects from the manufacturing process to events of transportation and exchange, social contexts of use and shifts in usage, ownership, or ascribed meaning and value. Similar principles determined the interview process, targeted toward recording past and current entanglements of the objects from the point of view of the participant. Emphasis was placed on the factors that rendered each object important enough for the owner to select it for the purpose of the interview, the ways it relates to their migratory experience, past life events, family history, and/or heritage.

The recorded material corpus varied widely and was ultimately grouped under six descriptive categories: kitchen ware/tableware, tools/appliances, home decoration, framed pictures/photobooks, textiles/knitting implements, and artwork/literature. While these groupings served mainly quantitative purposes, they allowed the identification of potential recurring patterns in the ways the volunteering individuals formed attachments to specific classes of artifacts. The latter becomes especially relevant in the case of the three teapots that function as the material base for this chapter: While there are otherwise no two objects of the same kind in the recorded corpus, the teapots stand out as the only class of artifacts across all categories that more than one individual identified as significant and personally selected to contribute to the project. They are also the only objects linked to this particular frame of reference (the Greek café). While some of the interviewees mentioned in passing that they have kept few plates and other serving/food consumption equipment from the cafés, the teapots were their object of choice to share during the interview process—an aspect that on its own is worthy of attention, as will be discussed below.

Teapots: The Objects, the People, the Stories

The three teapots belong to three individuals: Helen, Tony, and Vrettos (figs. 2, 3, and 4 respectively). Helen and Tony are Greek-Australians of Kytherian descent, who were born and raised in Australia, and relocated permanently to the island during the COVID-19 pandemic. Vrettos on the other hand is the son of a first-generation Greek-Australian return-migrant, born and raised in Greece. The teapots were all manufactured between the second and third quarters of the 20th century using the electroplating process, as indicated by the stamps on their underside. Tony's teapot (fig. 3) was

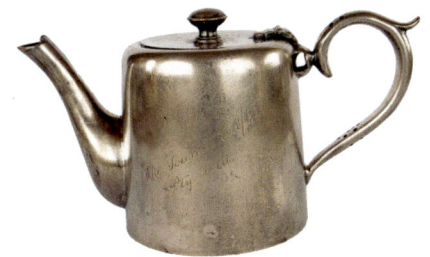

Fig. 2. EPNS teapot from The Tourist Café (courtesy of H. Tzortzopoulos; photograph by C. Marini).

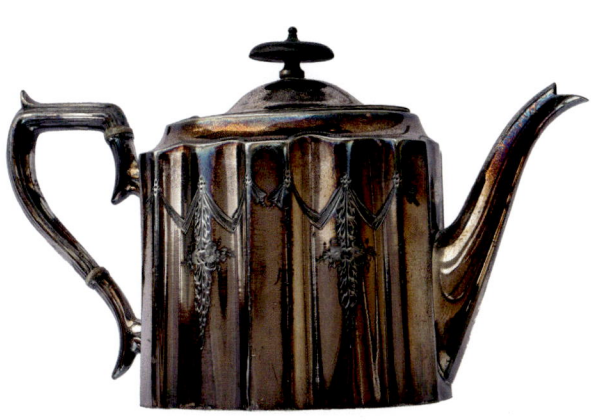

Fig. 3. EPBM teapot (courtesy of T. and S. Poulos; photograph by P. Diacopoulos).

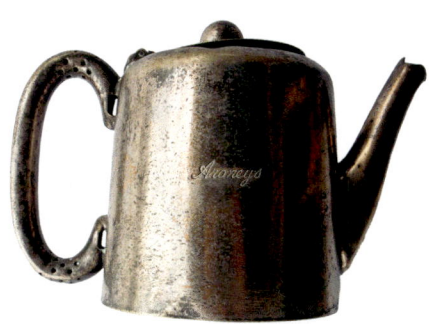

Fig. 4. EPNS teapot from Aroney's café (courtesy of V. Kypriotis; photograph by C. Marini).

made of Electroplated Britannia Metal (EPBM) in Sheffield, by the firm of James Deakin & Sons, while the teapots owned by Helen and Vrettos (figs. 2, 4) were made of Electroplated Nickel Silver (EPNS) in Sydney. The latter two vessels bear individualized branding of the establishments they were used in, The Tourist Café and Aroney's, respectively. The itineraries of the three vessels can be examined in three segments: the manufacturing process, their circulation and use in Australia during the 20th century, and their present-day status in domestic assemblages on Kythera.

Manufacture and Distribution

The manufacturer details engraved on the base of each teapot are the first source of information about the networks of relationships the objects were embedded in across the *chaîne opératoire*. All three vessels were produced in an industrial setting, using the electroplating process—a technology that was introduced in the 1830s.[13] The plating of a less valuable base metal, in our case Britannia metal and nickel silver, with a more precious one was a crucial step in reducing the cost of production of silver wares and achieving mass production. Albeit no longer considered groundbreaking by the second and third quarters of the 20th century, when the three teapots entered the cycle of circulation and use, the electroplating process is part of the employment of technological and scientific innovation in the service of the capitalist economy.[14]

Within the context of the factory, the teapots were entangled with the professional lives of people with different responsibilities and specializations across all stages of production, from the acquisition of the raw materials to the operation of the industrial machinery and the maintenance of the facilities. For that segment of their itineraries they were tied to the livelihood of factory workers, and their own efforts to establish or safeguard work rights. Long before they reached the consumer they were part of designing, advertising, and branding processes, and their distribution would have resulted in financial relationships between the producers and middlemen, salesmen, or even shipping companies, in the case of the teapot that was produced in Sheffield.

The two teapots made in Sydney (figs. 2, 4) additionally testify to the relational connections that developed between the manufacturer or vendor and the Kytherian owners of the establishments the teapots were purchased for. Both vessels were engraved with the names of the cafés they belonged to, indicating that they were specifically commissioned for this purpose by the store owners. The designation of the proprietor besides communicating the name of the establishment, reflects the interest of the owners for business branding. However, this investment was not necessarily possible for all vessels comprising the tea sets. Vrettos, one of our interviewees, owns a four-vessel set, of which only the teapot and the sugar bowl bear proprietary branding, while two creamers— made by the same manufacturer—are plain. The serving and pouring equipment was not necessarily purchased in a single order or by the same manufacturer. In the aforementioned set, for example, despite having common manufacturer details, the branding of the two specimens is not identical, with the use of cursive and first letter capitalization on the teapot, as opposed to all capitals on the sugar bowl, suggesting the purchase of the vessels in two different phases.

The Greek Café
The three teapots became incorporated, alongside a wide assortment of tablewares, equipment, and other goods, in the materiality of the Greek café, the most iconic aspect of Greek entrepreneurship in Australia. The introduction of the Greek café itself was a product of transnational mobility, onward migration, and the hybridization both entail. During the first wave of mass-migration from Greece, in the end of the 19th century, numerous Greeks, Kytherians among them, followed the transatlantic route to the United States and were absorbed in the food-catering industry. The interwar period saw many of them migrating onward to Australia, in search of new business opportunities and transferring their experience to a different market. They invested in previously Anglo-run businesses, like oyster saloons, equipping them with contemporary innovations, already popular in the US scene, like soda fountains and American-style ice cream.[15] Many of the new first-generation Greek migrants followed this business model and eventually more and more enterprises turned to the American-style drugstore/ milk bar model (figs. 5–7).

Greek-owned milk bars, soda and sundae parlors, generally grouped under the broader term of the Greek café, reshaped the Australian foodservice industry and became hubs of social life not only in urban centers but also in rural areas, where they often were the only available dining options.[16] Their pop-

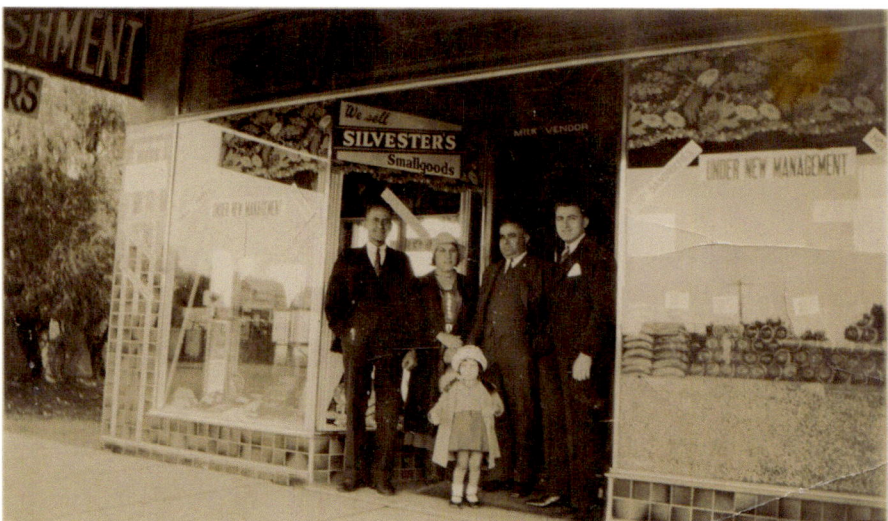

Fig. 5. Photograph of Greek
(Kytherian) storeowners,
Nyngan, central NSW, 1933
(photograph courtesy of H.
Castrisos).

Fig. 6 (opposite top). Niagara
Café, Gundagai, NSW, Aus-
tralia, ca. 1938 (photograph
courtesy J. Castrission; from
the In Their Own Image:
Greek-Australians, National
Project Archives).

Fig. 7 (opposite bottom).
California Café, Nyngan,
NSW, Australia, ca. 1939
(photograph courtesy C.
Kourt and J. Varvaressos;
from the In Their Own Image:
Greek-Australians, National
Project Archives).

ularity is effectively reflected in the phrase "I'll meet you at the
Greeks" that became common between the 1940s and 1960s.
They were a fusion of elements drawn from American food
business practices and preestablished consumption patterns
spread by British imperialism, reinterpreted by their Greek
owners to cater to the tastes of a local market on the road to
modernity.[17] Their cosmopolitan and American names, such
as Elysian, Golden Gate, Hollywood, Monterey, New York,
and Niagara, and their American-inspired aesthetics offered
the novelty of American dining (figs. 6, 7), while their menus
retained traditional Anglo- selections. All the while, they had
no overlap with either the Greek coffee culture nor with traditional Greek cuisine, the latter slowly appearing in the Australian restaurant scene only after the 1970s.

Within this culinary, social, and performative context, the
inclusion of tea as a served beverage—and the teapots themselves as serving vessels—catered to a distinctly Anglo-Aus-
tralian taste, stemming from the persistent popularity of the
British tea culture. The owners of the Greek cafés adapted
to a preestablished consumer practice that was born in the
sphere of British imperialism.[18] While tea-drinking habits
are culturally and socially diverse, the beverage had reached
globalized consumption through the East India Company
long before the floruit of the Greek cafés.[19] It had become an
affordable luxury, imbued with cultural values that in many
ways defined Englishness, crossing and at the same time reinforcing social boundaries.[20] Within these trajectories, the

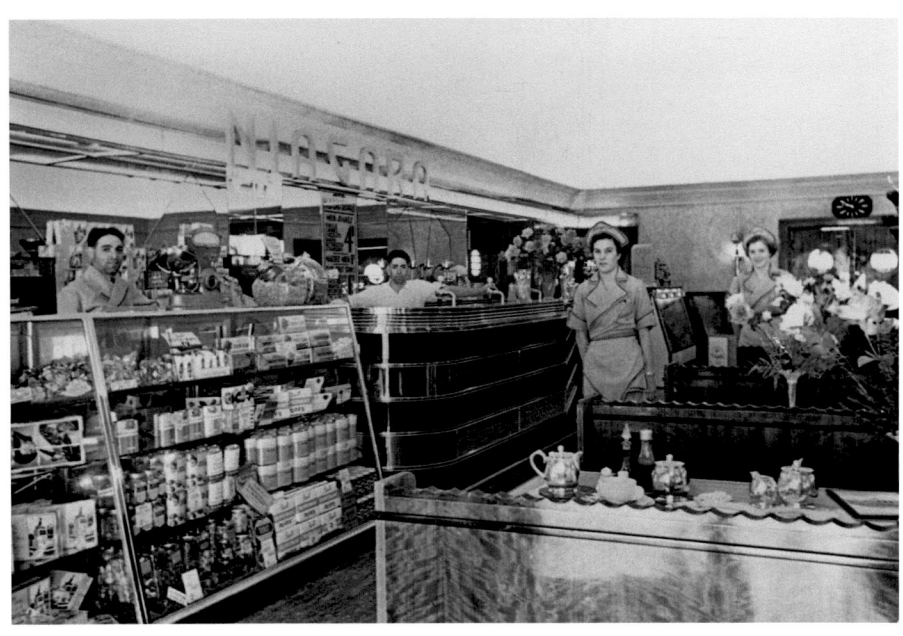

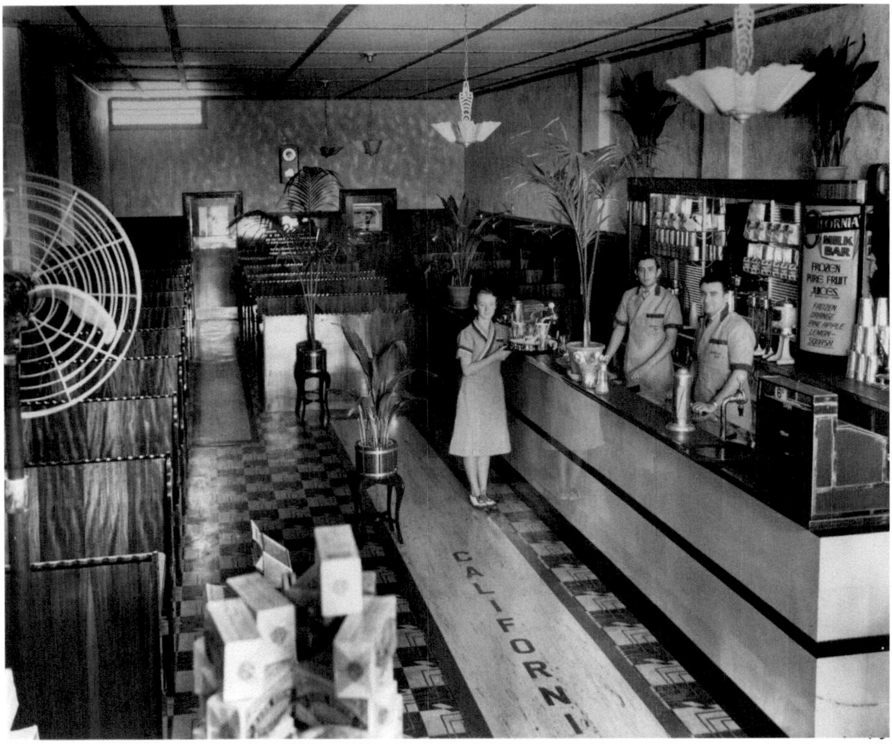

Greek cafés popularized and commodified the experience for the Australian clientele.

The use of electroplated teapots in particular not only corresponded to consumption trends of the time, but was also similarly entangled with class-related issues going back to Victorian times. As already mentioned, the emergence of electroplated wares in the first half of the 19th century was a decisive step toward the maximization of profit of the growing industrial economy. The reason behind their success is tied to the rise of the middle class in Victorian Britain.[21] A whole class of objects that previously held an exalted status, due to its association with aristocratic ideology and material practice, quickly became much less exclusive. Electroplated vessels appealed to aspiring members of society who could afford to emulate the upper-class tastes and habits, consuming commodities that at least in terms of style imitated the luxurious silverwares. As part of the assemblages of the Greek cafés, the three electroplated teapots catered to a nostalgia for elitist material practices of the past. This is particularly visible on Tony's teapot, which continues Victorian stylistic principles (fig. 3).

From Australia to Kythera
The history of ownership of each vessel assists to understand why the objects acquired new meanings and were not discarded after the original establishments they belonged to closed down. Helen's teapot comes from the café run by her parents, Tony's from a milk bar owned by one of his uncles, and Vrettos' teapot originates from his paternal uncle's business. They were passed down to their current owners as heirlooms, or were rediscovered after a period of disuse. Both Helen and Tony vividly remember childhood experiences in their families' cafés. Their recollections focus primarily on the meals, tastes, and smells of the cafés, and the family dynamics that developed in the stores. As Helen recounts: "We grew up in the café.… I remember when we wanted a meat pie or steak, we would go to the café and get a fresh batch." The bidirectional relation between notions of identity and food ways is crucial in comprehending the factors that contributed to the eventual incorporation of the teapots in their current owners' households.[22]

Even though their owners do not explicitly associate the vessels with the memories recounted in the oral interviews, the teapots appear to function as proxies for these memories, encapsulating emotions, events, and personal relationships. This can be effectively glimpsed from Tony's interview: "One of my uncles … started this place called the Niagara—he was one of the first in Australia to import an American soda fountain…. He was one of my favorite uncles, because he used to give me free drinks [laughs]. My godmother was fabulous. My godmother and godfather, they had another milk bar, and I used to have hot chocolates [there] all the time." The teapot, thus, triggers memories associated with not one, but two separate environments and family members, even though it originates only from the first of the two milk bars and is not actively involved in either of the recalled occasions.

As to why the teapots themselves, among the diverse equipment and furnishing of the stores, were the objects selected—consciously or not—to serve that purpose, we need to consider a combination of the formal characteristics of the vessels and matters of circumstance. The fact that two of the vessels bear the name of the establishments would have distinguished them among other material artifacts from the cafés, demonstrating in writing their relevance to family history and heritage. Their easily transportable character and the fact that they could easily find a use in a domestic context facilitated their transfer in a new setting of use, while the aesthetic value of silverwares and the good state of preservation of the items increased their appeal. On the other hand, opportunity and coincidence also played a role. Tony accidentally rediscovered the teapot, after inspecting property in the building that used to house his uncle's milk bar, while Vrettos came into possession of his tea set when other members of the family decided they no longer wanted it.

For the most recent segment of their itineraries all three teapots went through physical movement, from Australia to Kythera, which resulted in their inclusion in new social and performative contexts. The end of the 20th century encouraged a nonnegligible return-migratory flow from Australia, responsible for bringing Vretos's teapot to his hands, although the exact circumstances of its transportation are by now forgotten. The other two vessels accompanied their owners across long transnational journeys, following their international personal and professional lives, until they eventually settled on Kythera permanently during the COVID-19 pandemic. While deemed of emotional value, their owners no longer place emphasis on their utilitarian function. In two cases they have transformed into decorative items, placed in visible spots of their owners' homes. All three individuals note that they cherish the teapots for their symbolic associations with their ancestry, their own and/or their parent's country of origin, and their heritage, and they intend to pass them down to their children as heirlooms.

Conclusion

The presented itineraries of the three objects from Kythera, as outlined above, are strongly connected with the interplay of materiality and the conceptualizations of identity in imagined communities such as modern-day diasporas. The Greek café, which emerged as an amalgamation of different cultural elements in a globalized environment, became an iconic element of Greek Australiana and contributed to the construction of a shared transnational consciousness within the Greek-Australian migrant community. Besides the influence of these Greek immigrant businesses on Australian society, their impact on the migrant Greek communities was tremendous. The owners of Greek cafés anglicized their names, hired non-Greek staff, and served food disconnected from their own heritage, demonstrating that the executive choices involved in running these enterprises were part of a conscious business strategy. They provided employment to new immigrants and their families during the challenging transition of settling in their new country of residence and offered a place for them to socialize.

As such, Greek cafés and their material attributes were crucial in the creation of a tangible framework for the negotiation of the hybridized identities of the migrants at a communal and public level. They shaped intergenerational narratives that were mediated and communicated through shared material practices and imagery. The interpersonal relationships and social dynamics that developed within the context of the cafés were anchored and defined by food consumption patterns and the material assemblages of the stores, from furniture and decorations to serving equipment like the teapots themselves. These aspects, in addition to the pleasing design and the durability of the teapots, prompted previous and current owners to keep the vessels after they stopped being in fashion and the initial establishments declined. While the meanings ascribed to each artifact are dependent upon its distinct relational connections and the specific individual circumstances of its circulation, history of use, and transportation, all itineraries are marked by the shared narratives intertwined with the Greek cafés. In their current settings they are imbued with nostalgia and symbolism, carrying memories of successful business ventures, entrepreneurship, and adaptability.

Notes

[1] We wish to thank all volunteers, and especially V. Kypriotis, H. Tzortzopoulos, and T. and S. Poulos. Many thanks go to P. Diacopoulos and S. Biernath for the photo processing, and all researchers of the Finds Stories Project, especially K. Trimmis. The project has been supported by the EU Erasmus+ KA 2 scheme (grant number 2020-1-UK01-KA201-079065).

[2] Pratt 1978.

[3] For Kytherian migration in the centers of the Ottoman empire, see Kassimati 2021, 25–34.

[4] Gilchrist 1992, 95–222; Kassimati 2021, 65–73.

[5] For an overview of Greek migratory trajectories, see, e.g. Tamis 2005; Kardassis and Harlaftis 2006; Kitroeff 2006.

[6] For voluntary and forced migration, see, e.g., Fortier 2000; Basu and Coleman 2008; Yi-Neumann et al. 2022. For world diasporas, see e.g., Werbner 2000; Crang 2010.

[7] For possessions of first-generation migrants, see, e.g., Mehta and Belk 1991; Burrell 2008; Bertram 2010. For Greek-Australian migrants see Agutter et al. 2013. The 100th anniversary of the Lausanne Treaty has also generated significant recent interest in the materiality of Greek refugees, see, e.g., the digital exhibition Objects in Motion: What Objects Did the Refugees Who Came to Greece after August 1922 Bring with Them? (https://100objects.eie.gr/en/), organized by the Institute for Historical Research of the National Hellenic Research Foundation, which employs elements of the object-biographical approach in relation to possessions of Greek refugees from Asia Minor, Pontus, and Eastern Thrace. For domestic assemblages, see, e.g., Tolia-Kelly 2004; Walsh 2006; Barrett 2011; Savaş 2014; Marschall 2019.

[8] Mankekar 2002; Trimmis et al. 2021.

[9] E.g., Kourelis 2008; Brighton 2009; Hamilakis 2018; Martin 2023.

[10] Hahn and Weiss 2013; Joyce and Gillespie 2015. For an overview of theoretical advances see Bauer 2019.

[11] Hodder 2011, 2012, 2014; see also the posthumanist approach of Harris and Crellin 2018; Crellin and Harris 2021.

[12] Tsagarousianou 2004; cf. Anderson 2006.

[13] Raub 1993.

[14] Gleason 2001, 15–22.

[15] Risson 2014.

[16] For their thorough photographic documentation see Alexakis and Janiszewski 2016.

[17] Janiszewski and Alexakis 2003, 2020.

[18] Vogt-William 2011.

[19] Robins 2012, 146–48.

[20] Fromer 2008, 69–87.

[21] Gleason 2001, 30–33.

[22] Sutton 2001; Twiss 2007.

Works Cited

Agutter, K., E. Bouvet, D. Glenn, L. Leader-Elliott, C. Finnimore, D. Cosmini-Rose, and M. Palaktsoglou. 2013. "Migrants' Belongings: Preliminary Considerations of Greek and Italian Migrants' Travel Trunks in the Post-Second World War Period of Settlement to South Australia." *Modern Greek Studies* Special Issue:305–24.

Alexakis E., and L. Janiszewski. 2016. *Greek Cafés and Milk Bars of Australia*. Sidney: Halstead Press.

Anderson, B. 2006. *Imagined Communities: Reflections on the Origins and Spread of Nationalism*. Rev. ed. London: Verso.

Barrett, M. 2011. "The Memory of Objects: Eurasian Women (Re) Creating Identity and Belonging in the Post-Migratory Home." In *Imagining Home: Migrants and the Search for a New Belonging*, edited by D. Glenn, E. Bouvet, and S. Floriani, 102–21. Kent Town: Wakefield Press.

Basu, P., and S. Coleman. 2008. "Introduction: Migrant Worlds, Material Cultures." *Mobilities* 3:313–30. DOI: 10.1080/17450100802376753.

Bauer, A.A. 2019. "Itinerant Objects." *Annual Review of Anthropology* 48:335–52. DOI: 10.1146/annurev-anthro-102218-011111.

Bertram, L.K. 2010. "Public Spectacles, Private Narratives: Canadian Heritage Campaigns, Maternal Trauma and the Rise of the Koffort (Trunk) in Icelandic-Canadian Popular Memory." *Material Culture Review* 71:39–53.

Brighton, S. 2009. *Historical Archaeology of the Irish Diaspora: A Transnational Approach*. Knoxville: University of Tennessee Press.

Burrell, K. 2008. "Materialising the Border: Spaces of Mobility and Material Culture in Migration from Post–Socialist Poland." *Mobilities* 3: 353–73.

Crang, P. 2010. "Diasporas and Material Culture." In *Diasporas: Concepts, Intersections, Identities*, edited by K. Knott, and S. McLoughlin, 139–44. New York: Zed Books.

Crellin, R.J., and O.J.T. Harris. 2021. "What Difference Does Posthumanism Make?" *CAJ* 31:469–75. DOI: 10.1017/S0959774321000159.

Fortier, A.-M. 2000. *Migrant Belongings: Memory, Space, Identity.* Oxford: Berg.

Fromer, J.E. 2008. *A Necessary Luxury: Tea in Victorian England.* Athens: Ohio University Press.

Gilchrist, H. 1992. *Australians and Greeks, Vol. 1: The Early Years.* Rushcutters Bay: Halstead Press.

Gleason, M.E. 2001. "From Vulgarity to the Current Fashion: The Impact of Electroplating on Victorian Industry, Marketing, and Design." M.A. thesis, University of Glasgow.

Hahn, H.P., and H. Weiss, eds. 2013. *Mobility, Meaning and the Transformations of Things: Shifting Contexts of Material Culture through Time and Space.* Oxford: Oxbow.

Hamilakis, Y., ed. 2018. *The New Nomadic Age: Archaeologies of Forced and Undocumented Migration.* Sheffield: Equinox Publishing.

Harris, O.J.T., and R.J. Crellin, 2018. "Assembling New Ontologies from Old Materials: Towards Multiplicity." In *Rethinking Relations and Animism: Personhood and Materiality*, edited by M. Astor-Aguilera and G. Harvey, 55–74. Abingdon: Routledge.

Hodder, I. 2011. "Human-Thing Entanglement: Towards an Integrated Archaeological Perspective." *JRAI* 17:154–77. DOI: 10.1111/j.1467-9655.2010.01674.x.

———. 2012. *Entangled: An Archaeology of the Relationships between Humans and Things.* Malden: Wiley-Blackwell.

———. 2014. "The Entanglements of Humans and Things: A Long-Term View." *New Literary History* 45:19–36.

Janiszewski, L., and Alexakis, E. 2003. "American Beauties at the Niagara: The Marriage of American Food Catering Ideas to British-Australian Tastes and the Birth, Life and Demise of the Classic Australian 'Greek Cafe.'" In *Out There? Rural and Regional Conference*, edited by J. Goddard, 1–11. Sydney: National Trust of Australia.

———. 2020. "Café Ware Seduction." Paper read at the 23rd Symposium of Australian Gastronomy, Brisbane, Australia 17–20 July 2020. https://www.gastronomers.net/forum/organisers/session-3-dining-aesthetics-leonard-janiszewski-effy-alexakis.

Joyce, R.A., and S.D. Gillespie, eds. 2015. *Things in Motion: Object Itineraries in Anthropological Practice.* Santa Fe: SAR Press.

Kardassis, V., and G. Harlaftis. 2006. "Αναζητώντας της χώρες τις επαγγελίας: Ο απόδημος Ελληνισμός από τα μέσα του 19ου αιώνα ως το β' παγκόσμιο πόλεμο." In *Οι Έλληνες στη Διασπορά, 15ος–21ος αι.*, edited by I.K. Hassiotis, O. Katsiardi-Hering, and E.A. Ampatzi, 53–74. Athens: Hellenic Parliament.

Kassimati, K. 2021. *Μεταναστεύσεις από και προς τα Κύθηρα τον 20ο αιώνα: Κυθήριοι στην Αυστραλία, Αλβανοί στα Κύθηρα.* Athens: Gutenberg.

Kitroeff, A. 2006. "Η Μεταπολεμική μετανάστευση." In *Οι Έλληνες στη Διασπορά, 1505–2105 αι.*, edited by I.K. Hassiotis, O. Katsiardi-Hering, and E.A. Ampatzi, 75–91. Athens: Hellenic Parliament.

Kourelis, K., ed. 2008. *The Archaeology of Xenitia: Greek Immigration and Material Culture*. New Griffon 10. Athens: American School of Classical Studies.

Mankekar, P. 2002. "'India Shopping': Indian Grocery Stores and Transnational Configurations of Belonging." *Ethnos* 67:75–97. DOI: 10.1080/00141840220122968.

Marschall, S. 2019. "'Memory Objects': Material Objects and Memories of Home in the Context of Intra-African Mobility." *Journal of Material Culture* 24:253–69. DOI: 10.1177/1359183519832630.

Martin, S.C. 2023. "Materiality in Transit: An Ethnographic-Archaeological Approach to Objects Carried, Lost, and Gained during Contemporary Migration Journeys." *Journal of Social Archaeology* 23:3–24. DOI: 10.1177/14696053221144754.

Mehta, R., and R.W. Belk. 1991. "Artifacts, Identity, and Transition: Favourite Possessions of Indians and Indian Immigrants to the United States." *Journal of Consumer Research* 17:398–411.

Pratt, M. 1978. *Britain's Greek Empire: Reflections on the History of the Ionian Islands from the Fall of Byzantium*. London: Rex Collings.

Raub, C. 1993. "The History of Electroplating." In *Metal Plating and Patination: Cultural, Technical and Historical Developments*, edited by S. La Niece and P.T. Craddock, 284–90. Oxford: Butterworth-Heinemann. DOI: 10.1016/B978-0-7506-1611-9.50027-3.

Risson, T. 2014. "From Oysters to Olives at the Olympia Café: Greek Migrants and Australian Foodways." *Gastronomica* 14, no. 2:5–15. DOI: 10.1525/gfc.2014.14.2.5.

Robins, N. 2012. *The Corporation That Changed the World: How the East India Company Shaped the Modern Multinational*. 2nd ed. London: Pluto Press.

Savaş, Ö. 2014. "Taste Diaspora: The Aesthetic and Material Practice of Belonging." *Journal of Material Culture* 19:185–208. DOI: 10.1177/1359183514521922.

Sutton, D.E. 2001. *Remembrance of Repasts. An Anthropology of Food and Memory*. Oxford: Berg.

Tamis, A.M. 2005. *The Greeks in Australia*. Cambridge: Cambridge University Press.

Tolia-Kelly, D.P. 2004. "Locating Processes of Identification: Studying the Precipitates of Rememory through Artefacts in the British Asian Home." *Transactions of the Institute of British Geographers* 29:314–29.

Trimmis, K.P., D. Salapatas, and C. Marini. 2021. "Imaging the Materiality of a Diaspora: Recording the Biographies of Greek

Orthodox Church Buildings in London." *Anthropology Today* 37, no. 3:8–10. DOI: 10.1111/1467-8322.12651.

Tsagarousianou, R. 2004. "Rethinking the Concept of Diaspora: Mobility, Connectivity and Communication in a Globalised World." *Westminster Papers in Communication and Culture* 1:52–65. DOI: 10.16997/wpcc.203.

Twiss, K.C. 2007. "We Are What We Eat." In *The Archaeology of Food and Identity*, edited by K.C. Twiss, 1–15. Carbondale: University Carbondale.

Vogt-William, C. 2011. "Transcultural Tea Times: An Overview of Tea in Colonial History." In *Hybrid Cultures – Nervous States: Britain and Germany in a (Post)Colonial World*, edited by U. Lindner, M. Möhring, M. Stein, and S. Stroh, 127–49. Cross/Cultures 129. Leiden: Brill. DOI: 10.1163/9789042032293_008.

Walsh, K. 2006. "British Expatriate Belongings: Mobile Homes and Transnational Homing." *Home Cultures* 3:123–44. DOI: 10.2752/174063106778053183.

Werbner, P. 2000. "The Materiality of Diaspora—between Aesthetic and 'Real' Politics." *Diaspora: A Journal of Transnational Studies* 9:5–20. DOI: 10.1353/dsp.2000.0010.

Yi-Neumann, F., A. Lauser, A. Fuhse, and P.J. Bräunlein, eds. 2022. *Material Culture and (Forced) Migration: Materializing the Transient*. London: UCL Press.

Affective Gold: Exploring Materiality in Early Mycenaean Burials

Rachel Phillips

Abstract

This chapter examines the uses of gold in early Mycenaean burial contexts through the twin lenses of medium and materiality. It focuses on Grave Circle A at Mycenae (ca. 1700 B.C.E.), where gold foil was used to cover and adorn bodies, objects, and images. Using Shaft Graves IV and V as case studies, it argues that gold foil (in the form of masks, breastplates, and cutouts) was used to create a glittering image of the deceased and the assemblage, effecting a transformation from subject to object. Within this context, the body, or the skeleton, becomes the image, helped by the affective use of gold. The world of the dead is thus separated from the world of the living: the tension between appearance and reality not only emphasizes the desirability of the visual and material qualities of gold, but also serves to memorialize and heroize the deceased within the liminal space of the grave.[1]

Introduction

THE GOLD MASKS AND WEAPONS FROM GRAVE CIRCLE A at Mycenae remain some of the most famous objects ever uncovered on mainland Greece. More than 100 years after their discovery, and at least 3500 years after their original deposition, these assemblages still make an overwhelming, glittering impression. They are some of the first objects encountered in the National Archaeological Museum in Athens, but in their original contexts, they surrounded and adorned the dead, sealed away at the bottom of the grave. This study revisits these assemblages, focusing on the material relations of these burial contexts in order to better understand the various functions of gold within the early Mycenaean mortuary sphere.

From the start of the Late Bronze Age, around 1700 B.C.E., certain people on the Greek mainland were buried with hundreds or even thousands of objects made from precious materials (including gold) and embellished with figurative and abstract motifs. Aegean archaeologists typically interpret these assemblages in socioeconomic terms.[2] Within frameworks of conspicuous consumption, gold symbolizes the wealth of the deceased and the burying group, emphasizing their ability to access prestige resources, such as nonlocal objects and materials. Deposition not only fixes the value of the material, by removing it from circulation, but also legitimates the status of specific social groups.[3] These approaches, although valuable, overlook the significance of the physical properties of materials (including gold) as well as their specific uses within the mortuary sphere.[4]

This chapter aims to shift the focus of analysis from the exoticism and socioeconomic value of gold to its materiality. In doing so, it draws on several recent studies of gold within Minoan and Mycenaean archaeology. B. Legarra Herrero and M. Martinón-Torres, for example, have examined the uses and reuses of Early and Middle Minoan goldwork in cemeteries at Mochlos, Sissi, and Hagios Charalambos, attempting to reconstruct the life-histories of gold objects.[5] Rather than focusing on the economic value of gold, they emphasize processes of deposition, curation, and fragmentation. On the Greek mainland, E. Konstantinidi and N. Papadimitriou have reconstructed the gold-working techniques of Mycenaean craftsmen, exploring the different stages of production behind techniques such as granulation, foiling, and gold embroidery.[6] The role of craft specialization in the production of metal objects has also been examined by S. Aulsebrook, in her work on metals at Late Bronze Age Mycenae.[7]

Rather than treating gold objects as proxies for wealth and status, these authors emphasize the importance of the material properties of gold. In reconstructing the various decisions and motivations behind the creation and use of gold objects, they move beyond socioeconomic models that prioritize the nonlocal origin of gold above all else. Aulsebrook, for example, argues that the malleability and ductility of gold influenced its selection and use by Mycenaean craftsmen.[8] The visual qualities of gold, such as its color and shine, also played an important role, as C. Gillis has demonstrated in her analysis of the Mycenaean cemeteries at Dendra, Berbati, and Asine.[9]

Taking inspiration from these studies, this chapter prioritizes themes of material and materiality in its study of the

assemblages from Grave Circle A. It follows recent developments in Material Engagement Theory, where materiality
is defined in terms of the interactions between people and
objects.[10] L. Malafouris, for example, argues that meaning
emerges at specific moments within specific contexts, from
the entanglements between mind and matter, human cogni-
tion and material properties.[11] This chapter, more specifically,
understands materiality as the affective capacity of objects
and materials, in other words, as the impact of material properties on the viewer.[12] Although materiality represents just
one dimension of the burial assemblage, it is one that played
an important role in shaping the experiences of the mourners.[13] The perception and evaluation of certain material properties on the part of the mourners created new ways of seeing
and understanding. By focusing on the material properties of
gold, and by examining its specific uses within the mortuary
sphere, this study argues that it is overly simplistic to reduce
our interpretations of imported materials to issues of power
and conspicuous consumption. Status was not the only point
of interest for the people selecting and depositing these assemblages.

Grave Circle A at Mycenae

My chosen case studies are Shaft Graves IV and V in Grave
Circle A, in use at the beginning of the Late Bronze Age.
These graves are some of the earliest examples of truly os-
tentatious burials on the Greek mainland, representing the
emergence of new mortuary practices at the transition from
the Middle to the Late Bronze Age. Both graves contained
multiple burials with elaborate assemblages: Shaft Grave IV
contained five extended burials, each with their own assemblage, and Shaft Grave V contained three richly furnished
burials. Both also yielded commingled remains from earlier interments, meaning that the assemblages discussed here
represent the final context of the deposition, the final image
of the grave after multiple stages of arrangement and rear-
rangement. Although these graves are exceptional rather than
representative contexts, resulting from experimentation in
the mortuary arena at the transition from the Middle to the
Late Bronze Age, they nonetheless provide an excellent opportunity for the examination of the various forms and uses
of gold within specific early Mycenaean burial contexts, given
the wealth of their assemblages.

Shaft Graves IV and V were excavated by H. Schliemann in 1876, under the supervision of P. Stamatakis from the Greek Archaeological Service. Although Schliemann's original publications lack detail,[14] the discovery of Stamatakis's excavation diaries in the National Archaeological Museum of Athens has allowed for the reconstruction of the assemblages, including the placement of objects on and around the body of the deceased.[15] The skeletal remains have also been reexamined in recent years, so it is now possible to identify the genders and ages of most of the burials within Grave Circle A.[16] This study builds on these discoveries, in order to better understand the various functions of gold at Late Bronze Age Mycenae. How was gold used in the Shaft Graves? What did gold *do* for these assemblages and for these people?

My focus is the entanglement of bodies and objects within these burial contexts, as one way to illuminate the different roles that gold played within the early Mycenaean mortuary sphere. The relationship between bodies and objects has been overlooked by scholarship, which has traditionally prioritized objects over bodies, rather than understanding the assemblage as an integrated whole.[17] By contrast, my analysis here focuses on the material relations of the burial context, reconstructing the associations between objects and bodies within Shaft Graves IV and V before examining the potential impact of these associations for people at Late Bronze Age Mycenae. It examines the various ways in which the *materiality* of the assemblage relates to the *material reality* of the body.

All That Glitters Is Gold

This study begins in the Middle Bronze Age, in order to contextualize Shaft Graves IV and V within their broader chronological framework. In the Middle Bronze Age, people on the Greek mainland were buried in simple rectangular pits with few offerings. Ceramic vessels are common finds, but other objects and materials are rare. Gold is especially rare, attested at only one or two sites before the end of the Middle Bronze Age.[18] The earliest examples are the gold rings from the tumuli at Drachmani and Aphidna, dated (on the basis of the ceramic evidence) to the beginning of the period.[19] Another example is the gold pendant from the Middle Bronze Age settlement on the Aspis Hill at Argos, found close to the floor level of one of the houses. The pendant, according to the excavators, was not associated with any burial, suggesting that gold, at least in the Middle Bronze Age, was not restricted to the mortuary sphere.[20]

Toward the end of the Middle Bronze Age, gold starts to appear more frequently, deposited almost exclusively in mortuary contexts. Gold diadems, for example, have been found in graves at Corinth, Asine, and Argos.[21] In the Prehistoric Cemetery at Mycenae too, gold has been found in two graves dated to the end of the Middle Bronze Age.[22] The best precursor for the rich graves at Mycenae, however, is the Shaft Grave at Kolonna on Aegina. Among other objects, the grave contained metal weapons (fitted with gold adornment) and a gold diadem, deposited with the corpse of an adult male.[23] This assemblage seems to foreshadow developments in Grave Circle B at Mycenae, where most burials were accompanied by gold jewelry and ornaments, displayed on and around the body of the deceased. Grave Z, one of the earliest burials in Grave Circle B, contained the contracted skeleton of an adult man alongside six ceramic vessels and a large sword hilted with gold and ivory.[24] Grave Γ is the largest and richest grave in Grave Circle B, containing at least five burials alongside gold diadems and bands, bronze weapons, two metal vessels, over 50 ceramic vessels, and an amethyst seal.[25] One of the male skeletons was found with an electrum mask, placed next to the head rather than worn on the body.[26]

The explosion of gold objects in Grave Circle A, especially in the later graves, represents the culmination of these changes. Within Shaft Graves IV and V, gold is almost ubiquitous (fig. 1). It is the overriding visual impression from these assemblages, unifying the burials into one dazzling image. This image, however, is not homogenous. The burials in Grave Circle A are not simply hoards of valuable materials, but carefully curated assemblages, where gold is deposited in specific forms and in specific ways, mostly in relation to the body of the deceased.

Foiling the Body

The five burials in Shaft Grave IV were all furnished with gold objects and adornments.[27] Burials Ρ and Σ in Shaft Grave IV, identified as two probable female skeletons, wore gold funerary masks, with gold diadems on their foreheads.[28] Gold cutouts, perhaps originally sewn onto clothing, were found scattered on and around their bodies. Burial Ζ, an extended male skeleton about 30 years old, wore gold bands and

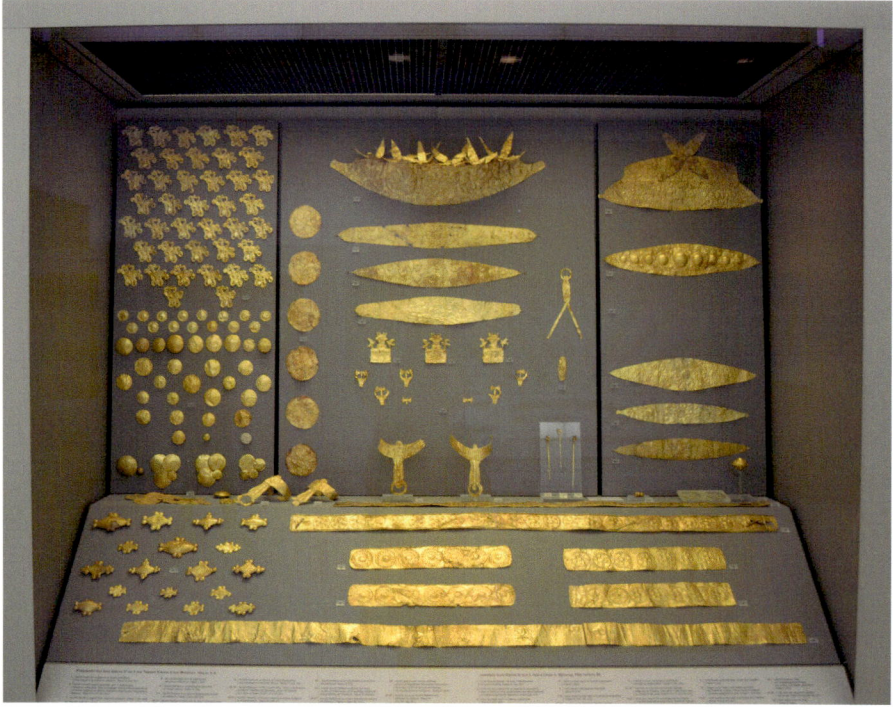

Fig. 1. The gold foil adorn-
ment from Shaft Grave V,
as displayed in the National
Archaeological Museum
in Athens (photograph
by author; courtesy of
the National Archaeo-
logical Museum, Athens, ©
ΥΠΟΥΡΓΕΙΟ ΠΟΛΙΤΙΣΜΟΥ/©
Hellenic Ministry of Culture/
Οργανισμός Διαχείρισης και
Ανάπτυξης Πολιτιστικών
Πόρων [ΟΔΑΠ]/Hellenic
Organization of Cultural
Resources Development
[H.O.C.RE.D.]).

diadems on his head and chest, with gold crosses on each of
his knees. Several swords, adorned with gold, were placed on
the left of the body, along with the famous lion-headed rhyton and the bull-headed rhyton. Over 100 gold-covered buttons were piled at his feet. The skeletal remains of Burial O,
identified as a 20-year-old man despite the poor preservation
of the bones, were mixed with gold bands and gold-covered
buttons. Swords and vessels (including five gold vessels) were
found at his feet. The best-preserved example from Shaft
Grave IV is Burial Π, an extended male skeleton about 30
years old. Burial Π wore a gold mask on his face and a gold
sheet across his chest, with gold foil bands on his forehead,
shoulders, arms, and legs. Gold foil buttons and cutouts were
found scattered around his body (fig. 2).

The three burials in Shaft Grave V represent the body in
similar fashion. Burial T, an extended male skeleton about 25
years old, wore a gold mask on his face (the so-called Mask
of Agamemnon) and a gold sheet across his chest, decorated
with interlinked spirals and two circles that seem to imitate
nipples. Gold bands were found on his forehead, shoulders,
arms, and legs, covering up the body almost entirely. Burial Φ

also wore a gold mask on his face, with gold bands and sheets across his body. Although no skeletal remains have survived from this burial, Stamatakis records the find-spots of these objects on and around the body.[29] Burial Y, the central burial in Shaft Grave V, identified as a probable adult male, was found disturbed, but associated finds from the fill include gold-covered buttons and bands. It is not too far-fetched to imagine that all three burials were originally covered by gold sheets and ornaments, carefully arranged on the body.

These coverings, in all likelihood, were made for the burial, and designed for the dead.[30] The masks, for example, have no eye-holes, and the gold sheets and bands are too flimsy to survive any kind of dynamic or active use. Instead, we should imagine that the body was dressed up in gold, covered in thin gold sheet, as part of the preparation of the corpse for burial. This kind of foiling parallels the use of gold to cover and conceal other objects and materials in Grave Circle A. Bone buttons and combs in Shaft Graves IV and V, for example, were wrapped in gold foil, made to look like gold, at least when viewed from the front. The rims and handles of silver vessels were covered with gold foil, on the shallow silver cup from Shaft Grave V, for example, or the Siege Rhyton from Shaft Grave IV. The swords and daggers from Grave Circle A were also adorned with gold foil. Their bronze blades were embellished with gold hilts, wrapped with gold bands, and inlaid with gold and silver imagery.

Taken together, these assemblages suggest that foiling played an important role in the mortuary sphere at Late Bronze Age Mycenae. Foiling was not restricted to objects, but applied to bodies too, creating new visual and sensory impressions of the burial. Although socioeconomic concerns, such as the desire to maximize the available material, must have influenced the development of foiling, the technique also exhibits an interest in the visual qualities of gold, its shine and durability. The tension between appearance and reality (the gold, after all, extends down only a few millimeters) does not seem to matter here, so long as objects and bodies *look* gold.

These gold coverings, in some cases, seem to imitate armor. The gold bands found with the male burials emulate the shoulder-straps and greaves known from Late Bronze Age warrior imagery,[31] and the gold sheets worn across the chest imitate breastplates. The choice of material, however, is not only unusual but also ineffectual. The gold foil, only a

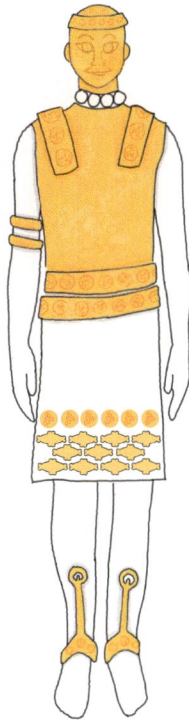

Fig. 2. Burial Π from Shaft Grave IV, as it might have looked with the gold sheets, bands, and cutouts displayed on the body (drawing by author).

few millimeters thick, offers no kind of protection. Instead, the emphasis is placed on display, on the appearance of the object over its practical function. However, in other cases, these gold coverings seem to imitate textiles. Gold bands and cutouts, sewn onto clothing, cover the body in layers stylized as drapery, where the various patterns and motifs could imitate the decoration of the fabric. It is important to note here that armor-adjacent foiling is reserved for the male burials in Shaft Graves IV and V whereas gold bands and cutouts were found with male and female burials, suggesting some level of gender differentiation in death.

Both male and female burials, however, were furnished with gold adornment. The assemblages in Shaft Graves IV and V seem designed to cover the body (at least the side facing the viewer) with gold. Only one body, the infant burial in Shaft Grave III, is covered on both sides, perhaps indicating different modes of viewing or handling during the funerary ceremony.[32] By adorning and covering the body, gold replicates the flesh of the deceased. The gold masks and breastplates are cut to the shape of the body and patterned with its physical features (eyes, mouth, nose, nipples). They become a second skin, blurring the boundaries between flesh and material. This "second skin" represents an important change from Grave Circle B, where the electrum mask from Grave Γ was found alongside the head of the deceased rather than on the face. In Grave Circle B, gold *represents* the body, but in Grave Circle A, gold *becomes* the body.

In making the body material, gold effects a transformation from subject to object.[33] The repeated use of gold, combined with the repeated practice of foiling, constructs visual and material associations between bodies and objects, making the body part of the assemblage. K. Harrell, in her work on Mycenaean weaponry, has emphasized the parallel treatment of swords and swordsmen in Grave Circle A, where both are dressed up in gold as part of their preparation for burial.[34] By constructing associations between objects and bodies, these assemblages not only elevate the status of the weapon to that of the warrior, as Harrell argues, but also incorporate the deceased into the assemblage, transforming the body into an object and marking the loss of the person within the world of the living.[35] Another example is the gold rosette attached on the forehead of the bull-headed rhyton, which seems to recall the gold diadems, embossed with rosettes, worn on the foreheads of the deceased.[36] The parallel treatment of the human body and the metallic bull aligns human with animal as well as body with object. The body is drawn into the materiality of the assemblage, where the transition from subject to object is enacted through specific material associations.

Gold also ensures that the body, and the assemblage, remain visible. During the funerary ceremony, the sparkle of the gold would stand out for people observing the preparation of the corpse or the procession to the grave, even from a distance.[37] During the process of deposition too, the shine of the gold would illuminate the assemblage while the objects were moved and arranged. The floor of Shaft Grave IV is several meters below ground, at the bottom of a rock-cut shaft. Presumably torches would have been required for the final arrangement, especially if the burial took place early in the morning or late at night. The shimmer of the gold under the flickering torchlight would produce an appropriately mystical atmosphere, just as the shine of the gold under the sunlight would produce a suitably dazzling impression. In addition, the durability of the gold ensures that this impression remained permanent, preserving an image of the deceased over time. The body, remade in gold, outshines the reality of decay and decomposition. Within this context, it is tempting to speculate on the ritual implications of gold, perhaps as symbolic of the successful transition to the afterlife or the achievement of immortality in death. This would coincide with contemporary Egyptian practices, where gold was used to represent the skin of the gods, reflecting their divine authority and immortality.[38]

Most significantly, however, gold immortalizes these individuals as the figures from the images in Grave Circle A. The warriors on the Lion Hunt dagger, for example, are characterized by their golden flesh, associated with the gold-covered bodies in the grave (fig. 3). On the Battle of the Glen signet ring, the bodies of the four warriors are united by the gold backdrop, marked out by the shine of the material (fig. 4). The repeated use of gold constructs associations (both material and conceptual) between the deceased individuals and the represented warriors. These associations transform the dead into the heroes and figures from stories, blurring the boundaries between the real and pictorial worlds. These associations do not necessarily reflect the biography of the individual (although this seems more likely for the burials with weapons)

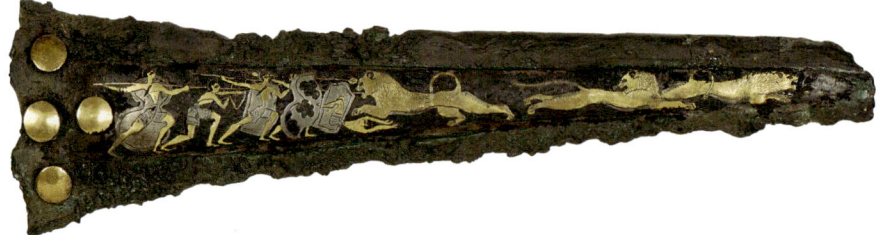

Fig. 3. Close-up view of the Lion Hunt dagger from Shaft Grave IV (NAM 394; courtesy of the National Archaeological Museum, Athens, © ΥΠΟΥΡΓΕΙΟ ΠΟΛΙΤΙΣΜΟΥ/© Hellenic Ministry of Culture/ Οργανισμός Διαχείρισης και Ανάπτυξης Πολιτιστικών Πόρων [ΟΔΑΠ]/Hellenic Organization of Cultural Resources Development [H.O.C.RE.D.]).

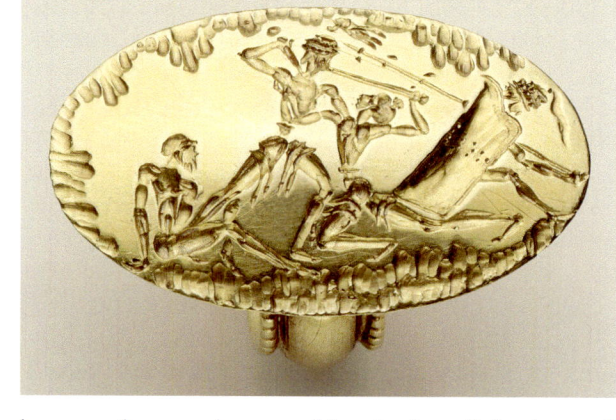

Fig. 4 (right). The Battle of the Glen signet ring from Shaft Grave IV (NAM 241). Length: 3.5 cm; width: 2.1 cm (courtesy of the National Archaeological Museum, Athens, © ΥΠΟΥΡΓΕΙΟ ΠΟΛΙΤΙΣΜΟΥ/© Hellenic Ministry of Culture/ Οργανισμός Διαχείρισης και Ανάπτυξης Πολιτιστικών Πόρων [ΟΔΑΠ]/Hellenic Organization of Cultural Resources Development [H.O.C.RE.D.]).

but contribute to the general heroization of the deceased, preserving specific images in the minds of the mourners. It is significant that this transformation seems restricted to the mortuary sphere in the early Mycenaean period. Deposition provides opportunities for the re-presentation of the body, creating new and shining images of the deceased, and separating the world of the dead from the world of the living.

Affective Gold

This study has examined the specific forms and uses of gold within Shaft Graves IV and V at Mycenae, in order to better understand the various functions of gold in the mortuary sphere. It has focused on the materiality of the burial assemblage as a way of exploring the impact of different material properties and associations within specific depositional contexts. In doing so, it has shown that gold was deposited in close association with the body in Shaft Graves IV and V. Gold coverings transformed the deceased into an image, blurring the boundaries between body and assemblage. The choice of material mediates the visual impression of the image, which is centered around the shine and durability of gold, its affective qualities. The creation of these body-images seems to be one of the key considerations behind the selection and deposition of objects within Grave Circle A. During the stage of prothesis, the laying out of the corpse with its accompanying objects would have facilitated the affective impact of the gold-covered dead, an impact also realized during the process of deposition and during the reopening of the grave for subsequent burials.[39]

These ideas complicate models that highlight conspicuous consumption as the key factor in the deposition of gold in early Mycenaean burial contexts. They problematize what gold artifacts actually did for people in the past, emphasizing the importance of the visual and sensory impressions created through the selection and deposition of specific materials. Although Shaft Graves IV and V are exceptional rather than representative examples, similar approaches can be productively applied to the use of gold and other imported materials within early Mycenaean burials more generally. By reexamining the material relations between objects and bodies within the mortuary sphere, and by focusing on the specificity of the deposition, it is possible to reframe these burials as complex processes of image-making and storytelling, centered around the figure of the deceased.

Notes

[1] This chapter builds on work conducted for my doctoral thesis at the University of Cambridge and I would like to thank my supervisors, Dr. Y. Galanakis and Professor C. Vout, for their support. This chapter was first delivered as a paper at the 2023 Annual Meeting for the Archaeological Institute of America, 6 January 2023, as part of a colloquium session titled *A Happy Medium: Media and Materiality in Ancient Art*. I would like to thank the panel organizers, R. Pare and R. Rumora, as well as Professor B. Burns, for their comments.

[2] E.g., Cavanagh and Mee 1998; Wright 2004; Eder and Zavadil 2021.

[3] E.g., Voutsaki 1997.

[4] See Brück and Fontijn 2013, 199–201.

[5] Legarra Herrero and Martinón-Torres 2021.

[6] Konstantinidi and Papadimitriou 2016.

[7] Aulsebrook 2022.

[8] Aulsebrook 2022, 101.

[9] Gillis 2015.

[10] The bibliography on materiality (and on Material Engagement Theory more specifically) is large. This chapter draws inspiration from Hodder 2011 and Malafouris 2013 in particular.

[11] Malafouris 2013, 35–43.

[12] Drawing on Morphy's (1994, 258) definition of aesthetics, which repurposes anthropological theories of the senses for archaeological purposes.

[13] See Boyd 2014, one of few studies that deals with materiality in Mycenaean burial contexts.

[14] Schliemann 1878.

[15] Konstantinidi-Syvridi and Paschalidis 2019.

[16] See the *Mycenae Revisited* series, especially Papazoglou-Manioudaki et al. 2010.

[17] See Moutafi and Voutsaki (2016, 781–82) for a similar critique.

[18] Laffineur 2010; Whittaker 2014.

[19] Philippa-Touchais and Touchais 2016, 286.

[20] Philippa-Touchais and Touchais 2016, 281.

[21] At Corinth, the gold diadem was found in Grave 3. At Asine, the diadem was found in Grave 1970–12. At Argos, gold was found in two graves in Tumulus E: a diadem from Grave 1(88) and three gold foil ornaments from Grave 5(92).

[22] Alden 2000. PC'39 Grave III contained five gold ornaments in the shape of spirals; Area Γ Grave 11 contained two gold disks, perforated at the edge so possibly used as earrings.

[23] Gauß 2021, 519. See also Kilian-Dirlmeier 1997 on the assemblage.

[24] Mylonas 1973, 102–5; Dietz 1991, 116–17.

[25] Mylonas 1973, 43–82; Dietz 1991, 108–11.

[26] Mylonas 1973, 47. Dickinson associates the mask with one of the female burials, on the basis of its similarity to the masks worn by the female burials in Shaft Grave IV (Dickinson et al. 2012, 177).

[27] My descriptions here are based on Dickinson (1977, 46–49) and Paschalidis (2018), with reference to the publication of these assemblages in Karo 1930. I follow Stamatakis's designations for the burials in Shaft Graves IV and V, as recorded in his excavation diaries.

[28] As above, the osteological analysis for Shaft Graves IV and V was undertaken as part of the *Mycenae Revisited* project, by A. Nafplioti and J.H. Musgrave; see Papazoglou-Manioudaki et al. 2010. Note that the identification of Burial P remains uncertain, although Konstantinidi and Paschalidis (2019) argue that both Burials P and Σ are female burials.

[29] Dickinson et al. 2012, 179.

[30] Whittaker 2014, 170, 172.

[31] Whittaker (2014, 161–62) suggests that these bands could be shield-straps.

[32] There is only evidence for one infant burial in Shaft Grave III,

so the gold sheets must have covered the front and back of the body (Papazoglou-Manioudaki et al. 2010, 161).

[33] Malafouris (2015, 306) notes the transition from self-as-subject to social self-as-object in Grave Circle A; see also Voutsaki (2010, 2012) on the fusion of subject to object in the Mycenae Grave Circles through processes of exchange and consumption.

[34] Harrell 2012, 802–4.

[35] See also Malafouris 2008 on the relationship between Mycenaean sword and swordsman.

[36] See Ramé 2022 on the wearing of diadems in the Aegean Bronze Age more generally.

[37] Boyd (2014) makes this point with reference to the gold seals from Tholos 2 at Routsi.

[38] Gates (1989, 217) suggested direct influences from Egypt on the use of gold in the Shaft Graves, but other comparanda are also plausible (Whittaker 2014, 175).

[39] Boyd (2014, 198) has reconstructed the stages of the early Mycenaean funeral, including prothesis, deposition, and subsequent reopenings.

Works Cited

Alden, M. 2000. *The Prehistoric Cemetery: Pre-Mycenaean and Early Mycenaean Graves*. Well Built Mycenae 7. Oxford: Oxbow Books.

Aulsebrook, S. 2022. "Forging Ahead or Foiled Again? A New Direction for Cross-Craft Analysis with Case Studies from Late Bronze Age Metalworking in the Aegean." *Sympozium Egejskie: Papers in Aegean Archaeology 3*, edited by S. Aulsebrook, K. Żebrowska, A. Ulanowska, and K. Lewartowski, 99–112. Turnhout: Brepols.

Boyd, M.J. 2014. "The Materiality of Performance in Mycenaean Funerary Practices." *WorldArch* 46:192–205. DOI: 10.1080/00438243.2013.879045.

Brück, J., and D. Fontijn. 2013. "The Myth of the Chief: Prestige Goods, Power and Personhood in the European Bronze Age." In *The Oxford Handbook of the European Bronze Age*, edited by H. Fokkens and A. Harding, 197–215. Oxford: Oxford University Press. DOI: 10.1093/oxfordhb/9780199572861.013.0011.

Cavanagh, W.G., and C. Mee. 1998. *A Private Place: Death in Prehistoric Greece*. SIMA 125. Jonsered: Paul Aström.

Dickinson, O.T.P.K. 1977. *The Origins of Mycenaean Civilisation*. SIMA 49. Göteborg: Paul Åström.

Dickinson, O.T.P.K., L. Papazoglou-Manioudaki, A. Nafplioti, and A.J.N.W. Prag. 2012. "Mycenae Revisited Part 4: Assessing the New Data." *BSA* 107:161–88. DOI: 10.1017/S0068245412000056.

Dietz, S. 1991. *The Argolid at the Transition to the Mycenaean Age: Studies in the Chronology and Cultural Development in the Shaft Grave Period.* Copenhagen: National Museum of Denmark.

Eder, B., and M. Zavadil, eds. 2021. *(Social) Place and Space in Early Mycenaean Greece: International Discussions in Mycenaean Archaeology, October 5–8, 2016, Athens.* Mykenische Studien 35. Vienna: Austrian Academy of Science Press.

Gates, C. 1989. "Iconography at the Cross-Roads: The Aegina Treasure." In *Transition: Le monde égéen du bronze moyen au bronze recent; Actes de la Deuxième Rencontre Internationale de l'Université de Liège (18–20 avril 1988),* edited by R. Laffineur, 215–24. Aegaeum 3. Liège: Université de Liège.

Gauß, W. 2021. "Kolonna on Aigina: The Development of a Fortified Middle and Early Late Bronze Age Settlement." In *(Social) Place and Space in Early Mycenaean Greece: International Discussions in Mycenaean Archaeology, October 5–8, 2016, Athens,* edited by B. Eder and M, Zavadil, 517–36. Mykenische Studien 35. Vienna: Austrian Academy of Science Press.

Gillis, C. 2015. "A Colourful Death. A Study of the Social Life of Colours in Late Bronze Age Grave Goods." In *Mycenaeans Up to Date: The Archaeology of the North-Eastern Peloponnese; Current Concepts and New Directions,* edited by A-L. Schallin and I. Tournavitou, 515–29. Stockholm: Swedish Institute in Athens.

Harrell, K. 2012. "The Weapon's Beauty: A Reconsideration of the Ornamentation of the Shaft Grave Swords." In *Kosmos: Jewellery, Adornments and Textiles in the Aegean Bronze Age: Proceedings of the 13th International Aegean Conference, Danish National Research Foundation's Centre for Textile Research, 21–26 April 2010,* edited by M.-L. Nosch and R. Laffineur, 799–804. Aegaeum 33. Leuven: Peeters.

Hodder, I. 2011. "Human-Thing Entanglement: Towards an Integrated Archaeological Perspective." *JRAI* 17:154–77. DOI: 10.1111/j.1467-9655.2010.01674.x.

Karo, G. 1930. *Schachtgräber von Mykenai.* Munich: F. Brückmann.

Kilian-Dirlmeier, I. 1997. *Das mittelbronzezeitliche Schachtgrab von Ägina.* Kataloge vor- und früh- geschichtlicher Altertümer 27. Mainz: Philipp von Zabern.

Konstantinidi, E., and N. Papadimitriou. 2016. "Technological Study and Interpretation of Rhomboid Accessories from Grave Circle A, Mycenae." In *RA-PI-NE-U: Studies on the Mycenaean World Offered to Robert Laffineur on the Occasion of His 70th Birthday,* edited by J. Driessen, 245–62. Louvain-La-Neuve: Presses Universitaires de Louvain.

Konstantinidi-Syvridi, E., and K. Paschalidis. 2019. "The Unacknowledged Panayotis Stamatakis and His Invaluable Contribution to the Understanding of Grave Circle A at Mycenae." *AR* 65:111–26. DOI: 10.1017/S0570608419000061.

Laffineur, R. 2010. "Jewellery." In *The Oxford Handbook of the Bronze Age Aegean*, edited by E. Cline, 443–54. Oxford: Oxford University Press.

Legarra Herrero, B., and M. Martinón-Torres. 2021. "Heterogeneous Production and Enchained Consumption: Minoan Gold in a Changing World (ca. 2000 BCE)." *AJA* 125:333–60.

Malafouris, L. 2008. "Is It 'Me' or Is It 'Mine'? The Mycenaean Sword as a Body-Part." In *Past Bodies: Body-centered Research in Archaeology*, edited by J. Robb and D. Borić, 115–23. Oxford: Oxbow Books.

———. 2013. *How Things Shape the Mind: A Theory of Material Engagement*. Cambridge: MIT Press.

———. 2015. "How Did the Mycenaeans Remember? Death, Matter, and Memory in the Early Mycenaean World." In *Death Rituals, Social Order and the Archaeology of Immortality in the Ancient World*, edited by C. Renfrew, M.J. Boyd, and I. Morley, 303–14. Cambridge: Cambridge University Press. DOI: 10.1017/CBO9781316014509.019.

Morphy, H. 1994. "Aesthetics across Time and Place: An Anthropological Perspective." *CAJ* 4:257–60.

Moutafi, I., and S. Voutsaki. 2016. "Commingled Burials and Shifting Notions of the Self at the Onset of the Mycenaean Era (1700–1500 BCE): The Case of the Ayios Vasilios North Cemetery, Laconia." *JAS Reports* 10:780–90. DOI: 10.1016/j.jasrep.2016.05.037.

Mylonas, G.E. 1973. *Ο ταφικὸς κύκλος Β τῶν Μυκηνῶν*. 2 vols. Athens: Βιβλιοθήκη τῆς ἐν Ἀθηναῖς Ἀρχαιολογικῆς Ἑταιρείας.

Papazoglou-Manioudaki, L., A. Nafplioti, J.H. Musgrave, and A.J.N.W. Prag. 2010. "Mycenae Revisited Part 3: The Human Remains from Grave Circle A at Mycenae; Behind the Masks; A Study of the Bones from Shaft Graves I–V." *BSA* 105:157–224.

Paschalidis, K. 2018. "Shaft Grave IV in Grave Circle A: New and Unexpected Light on a Very Old Story." Paper read at the Mycenaean Seminar, 16 May, London.

Philippa-Touchais, A., and G. Touchais. 2016. "Glow in the 'Dark': A Gold Pendant from a Middle Helladic Settlement (Aspis, Argos)." In *RA-PI-NE-U: Studies on the Mycenaean World Offered to Robert Laffineur on the Occasion of His 70th Birthday*, edited by J. Driessen, 275–93. Louvain: Presses Universitaires de Louvain.

Ramé, B. 2022. *Coiffures et parures de tête en Égée à l'âge du Bronze*. Louvain: Peeters.

Schliemann, H. 1878. *Mycenae: A Narrative of Researches and Discoveries at Mycenae and Tiryns.* New York: Scribner.

Voutsaki, S. 1997. "The Creation of Value and Prestige in the Aegean Late Bronze Age." *Journal of European Archaeology* 5, no. 2: 34–52. DOI: 10.1179/096576697800660285.

———. 2010. "Agency and Personhood at the Onset of the Mycenaean Period." *Archaeological Dialogues* 17:65–92. DOI: 10.1017/S1380203810000097.

———. 2012. "From Value to Meaning, from Things to Persons: The Grave Circles of Mycenae Reconsidered." In *The Construction of Value in the Ancient World*, edited by G. Urton and J. Papadopoulos, 112–37. Cotsen Advanced Seminars 5. Los Angeles: Cotsen Institute of Archaeology Press.

Whittaker, H. 2014. *Religion and Society in Middle Bronze Age Greece.* Cambridge: Cambridge University Press.

Wright, J. 2004. "The Emergence of Leadership and the Rise of Civilisation in the Aegean." In *The Emergence of Civilisation Revisited*, edited by J.C. Barrett and P. Halstead, 64–89. Oxford: Oxbow Books.

A Niche Medium: Medial Properties of Façade Statuary in Roman Ephesus

Roko Rumora

Abstract

Aedicular façades are among the most complex display spaces for statues employed in the Roman Imperial period. Consisting of multiple rows of superimposed statue-filled aediculae and niches, such façades decorated a variety of public buildings, and were especially popular in Roman Asia Minor. Scholarship has tended to focus on the architectural design of these structures, their function, or the iconographic programs of their statuary. This chapter presents two case studies from the city of Ephesus, the theater (85 C.E.) and the Library of Celsus (ca. 120 C.E.), in support of the argument that aedicular façades were sites of intermedial and intramedial play.

The case studies demonstrate how seemingly banal medial properties of statues, such as their ability to stand freely in open space, could become charged with additional agency when those statues were juxtaposed with objects visibly lacking those properties. At the same time, as (literal) carriers of meaning, aedicular façades can be productively understood as a medium of communication in their own right. Demonstrating a sharp awareness of medium-specific properties of statuary, the patrons of Ephesian façades accentuated the physicality of statues as objects; in doing so, they found novel ways of making visible the performative relationships that characterize euergetism in Roman Asia Minor.[1]

Introduction

Roman sculpture of the Late Republican and Early Imperial period is marked by an increased integration of statues into architecture following principles of axial symmetry.[2] Representative of this development are the so-called aedicular façades, multistory structures characterized by rows of statue niches and aediculae.[3] While aedicular façades first appeared during the Augustan period as the stage façades (*scaenae frontes*) of Roman theaters, they were also employed in other monumental civic structures, and became especially favored by civic benefactors in the cities of Asia Minor during the first and second centuries C.E.[4] Rather than having a structural relationship with the interior behind them, these façades were more like columnar screens, whose organizing principles could be endlessly varied, giving each façade a unique architectural rhythm. Recognizing the façade patron's freedom to combine projecting and receding parts, the following investigation draws attention to the way Roman aedicular façades articulated relationships between their own architecture and the statues they housed in their niches and aediculae.

Statue-filled façades were seen by Roman audiences accustomed to finding unstated meaning in the relationships between individual statues, their bases, and their built surroundings.[5] In the cities of the Roman Empire, this attentiveness could be cultivated through the declamations of skilled orators, frequently delivered in front of statue-filled theatrical façades, and often explicitly inviting reflection on the surrounding decoration.[6] Such interpretive attitudes could also evolve organically within communities; well into the late Roman period, theater-goers in Antioch noticed relationships of proximity between statues on the façade of a *scaenae frons* and even developed imaginative stories that retrospectively explained their juxtaposition.[7] Roman aedicular façades can therefore be seen as multimedia complexes that make visible both the intermedial and the intramedial relationships between sculpture and architecture.

The following remarks, preliminary in nature, respond to a revived scholarly interest in the concept of artistic medium and its applicability to premodern material cultures. Sometimes treated as a shorthand for the physical support of an image and at other times as a specific technique for producing said image, *medium* is a term with complex historiographic baggage.[8] In modernist art history, the concept is closely associated with the midcentury critic C. Greenberg and his advocacy of medium-specificity, or the "self-reflexive attention to an art form's material support."[9] Perhaps because scholars of the ancient world are "less tired, bored and scarred by the modernist debates around medium-specificity," the notion of medium has in recent years been productively combined with theories of materiality developed by theoretical archaeology, leading to new ways to think about ancient practices of mediation.[10]

Two case studies from Roman Ephesus, the city's theater (85 C.E.) and the Library of Celsus (ca. 120 C.E.), demonstrate how a sensitivity to the medium-specific properties of freestanding statuary allowed benefactors to draw attention to the *thingness* of statues, as physical objects entangled in the performative relationships of civic benefaction.[11] For present purposes, medium-specific properties can be defined as those perceptible aspects of a crafted object that stem from its being executed in a particular artistic medium. For example, having an (inscribed) base is a medium-specific property of freestanding statuary: a standing figure requires a base *because* it is produced as a statue, whereas a painting or a relief of that same figure would not *require* a base underfoot.

However, medium-specific properties are not without semantic connotations of their own. When figures in paintings or reliefs *do* stand on bases, this is not necessarily because they are meant to depict existing statues.[12] Instead, providing a relief-carved figure with a base allows one medium to perform the work of another: a relief, in this instance, gains access to the performative connotations of "putting someone up on a pedestal" that would otherwise belong only in the realm of large, freestanding statuary.[13] This is the kind of intermedial play that P. Stewart has dubbed statuesque.[14] If a relief can be made to perform the work of a freestanding statue, can a building do the same? What would it mean to erect a building as if it were a statue? Aedicular façades offer an opportunity to explore these issues, precisely because they are both a logical part of a building, while also serving as the framework holding up a statue.[15] The statue-filled façades are themselves a kind of medium, an in-between space where conventions and expectations may be upturned.

The Theater

The *scaenae frons* of the Ephesian theater (fig. 1) was articulated in rows of projecting aediculae and receding niches suitable for housing statuary.[16] The three-story stage façade was built in 85 C.E. and dedicated to Artemis of Ephesus and Domitian by the city of the Ephesians.[17] Over a dozen surviving statues, ranging from statuettes of divinities to colossal imperial portraits, are associated with a display somewhere on the façade, yet the lack of precisely recorded findspots presents significant challenges to study.[18] It is almost certain that the niches and aediculae of the Domitianic façade would

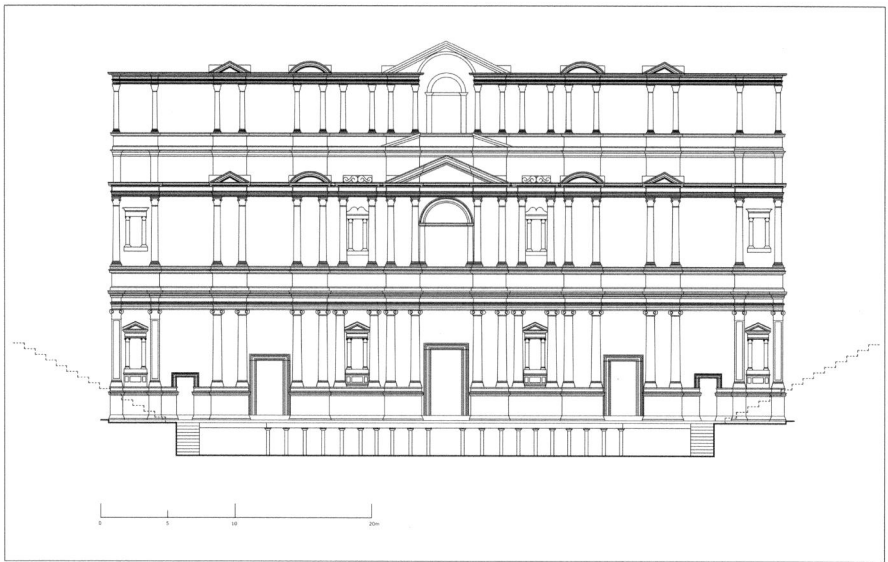

Fig. 1. Elevation drawing of
the theater façade in Ephesus
(Krinzinger and Ruggendorfer
2017, 444 fig. 15, after Öztürk
2010).

have been filled over time, with additions as late as the fourth century C.E.[19]

While most of the surviving statues from the Ephesus theater are carved fully in the round, at least four represent life-size figures with raised arms whose backs were articulated as architecturally embedded pillars (fig. 2).[20] Two of the better-preserved figures represent Amazons, and a third shows a youthful satyr. The fourth statue is known only through a fragment of a torso with an elevated shoulder; it, too, may have been an Amazon.[21] Although the exact display position of these pillar-backed figures on the *scaenae frons* is not known, dowel holes on the sides and upper surfaces of their pillars unmistakably characterize them as architectural, rather than freestanding sculpture.[22] They have been stylistically dated to the Antonine period and must have been part of a substantial renovation of the stage undertaken during that time.[23]

While the categories of *freestanding* and *architectural* sculpture are modern terms of scholarship, the underlying distinction—between statues that can be freely moved and those that are embedded into buildings—is one that was recognizable to Roman viewers. Vitruvius, in his discussion of the origins of caryatid statuary (*De arch.* 1.5), makes this explicit, by saying that architects need to have an explanation ready when asked why they employed statues carrying architectural

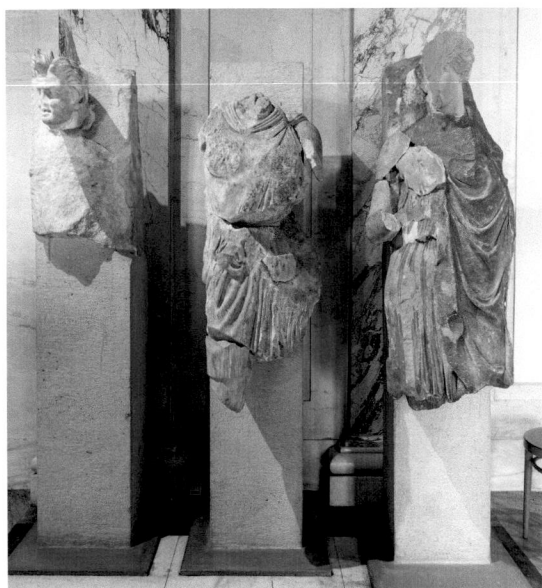
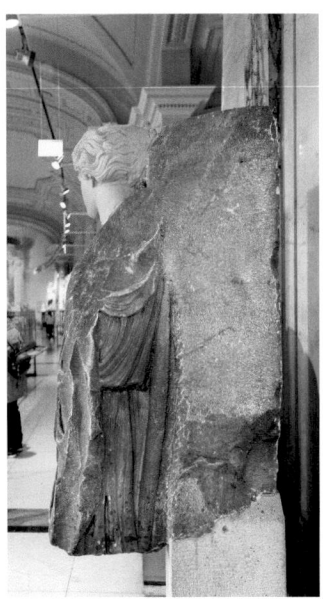

Fig. 2. Three pillar-backed figures from the theater in Ephesus. Vienna, Kunsthistorisches Museum I 834, I 1615, I 1616 (© Kunsthistorisches Museum Vienna, photograph by the author).

entablatures on their heads. The explanation Vitruvius offers as an origin story explains caryatids as statues of women from Caryae whose load-bearing role was a punishment for their siding with the Persians. It is important to note that, although he describes caryatids as part of a building, Vitruvius nevertheless identifies them using the standard vocabulary for freestanding statues (*statuas*).[24] In fact, the entire story of the women's punishment is predicated on viewers still thinking of them as such, as statues that were robbed of one of the most characteristic medial properties of in-the-round statuary—their mobility. For Vitruvius, the *loss* of this mobility was central to the caryatids' interpretation: it is because the sculpted women are subordinated to the building *literally* that they can be seen as subordinated *figuratively*—as symbols of eternal servitude.

The pillar-backed figures similarly performed their subordination to the architecture of the theater stage, with their arms raised above head at least hinting at a load-bearing role. In choosing to employ such figures, the designers of the Ephesian stage were reaching back to an element of Hellenistic theatrical architecture that predated the invention of the Roman *scaenae frons*.[25] Embedded among the niches and aediculae of a *scaenae frons*, however, these figures drew attention to precisely the medial property they lack—the mobility of freestanding statues lifted into position on the façade. Not only do the Amazons and satyr therefore *belong* to the building and appear inextricable to its very nature, but their positioning in the façade stands outside of time—they have been there for as long as the building has been there. Through the inclusion of Amazons as subjects, this reference to antiquity was given a site-specific character, as Amazons held an important place in the earliest history of Ephesus.[26] By contrast, the truly freestanding statues that would come to populate the façade's available niches and aediculae get to be perceived as a series of *acts* of deposition. As a sequence of individual objects placed into difficult-to-reach positions—once the architectural framework had already been completed—the freestanding statues emphasize not only the distinct temporality of their own display, but also the agency of their displayer.

The social value of emphasizing the agency involved with lifting statues into position could be considerable, for it allowed the benefactors to focus public attention on the costliness of their efforts, an aspect frequently mentioned in dedicatory inscriptions.[27] One example that demonstrates the extent to which this effort was seen as worthwhile is the seated nude statue of a bearded, mature male, dated to the Antonine period—one of the few statues from the theater with a precise findspot (fig. 3). Excavated in the middle of the stage, it likely occupied the central display space on one of the façade's upper stories.[28] Although the figure has long been associated with a base for a statue of the Demos of Ephesus, found in the central passageway below the stage, the statue's identification warrants further research.[29] The hairstyle, beard, and middle-aged musculature suggest a mature male deity, such as Poseidon or Zeus. The latter is a particularly intriguing possibility, as there is a long tradition of Ephesian coin issues depicting a seated Zeus holding a statuette of the Artemis of Ephesus.[30]

The seated figure is notable for the numerous dowel holes and pinholes distributed across the entire body, many of which can best be interpreted as signs of repairs undertaken in antiquity. The elevation of the repaired seated figure into its position on the second or third story would have required significant efforts and labor costs, including setting up scaffolding directly on the stage floor. Literary sources attest that the sight of such scaffolding contributed to the perceived grandeur of the undertaking.[31] Through their juxtaposition with pillar-backed figures displayed elsewhere on the façade, the mobility of such repaired

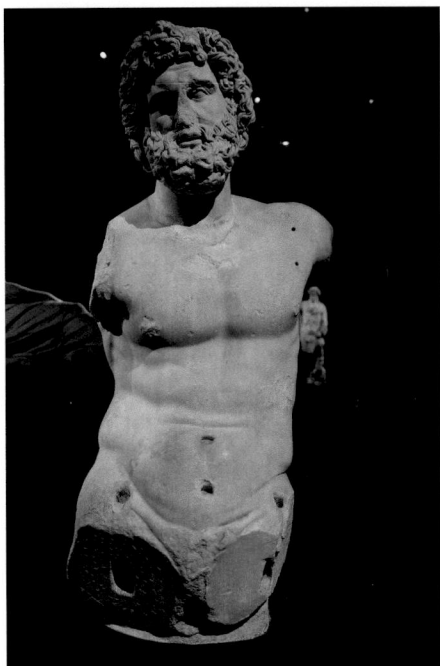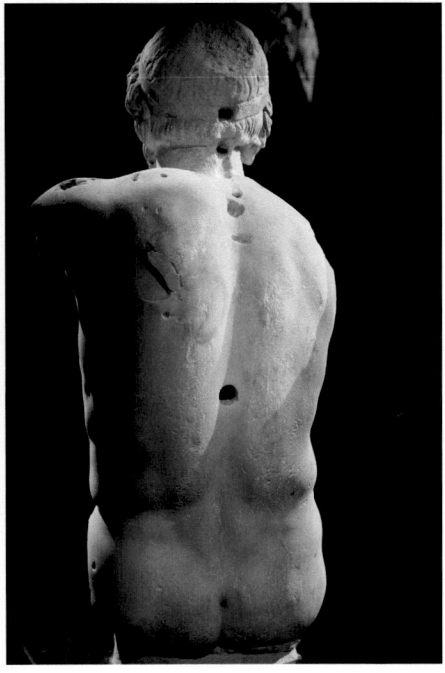

Fig. 3. Statue of a bearded male with signs of extensive repair, from Ephesus theater. Istanbul, Archeological Museum 2454 (photograph by the author, with kind permission of the Istanbul Archaeological Museum).

figures could become noticeable as a distinct trait, helping to emphasize, among other things, the fact of their repair. In several Roman theater façades, repaired statuary was prominently displayed in ways that highlighted, rather than concealed, the fact that the objects had once been broken.[32] As M. Aurenhammer has argued in her study of the Ephesian seated statue, its repairs may have been conspicuous, including visible metal clamps and marble patches.[33] Inscriptions elsewhere in the Ephesus theater suggest that its patrons proudly emphasized ongoing repairs.[34] Once deposited into niches and aediculae on a tall façade, and especially if juxtaposed with architecturally subordinated figures, the autonomous stillness of freestanding figures such as the seated male nude appears as the end result of a costly process of *moving*—a process made possible by the generosity of the benefactor.

The Library of Celsus

If the medial games of the Ephesian *scaenae frons* relied on viewer expectations regarding the mobility of statues, the façade of the nearby Library of Celsus (fig. 4) played with epigraphic conventions specific to the medium of statuary.[35] The building, completed about 120 C.E., is a library and *heroon*

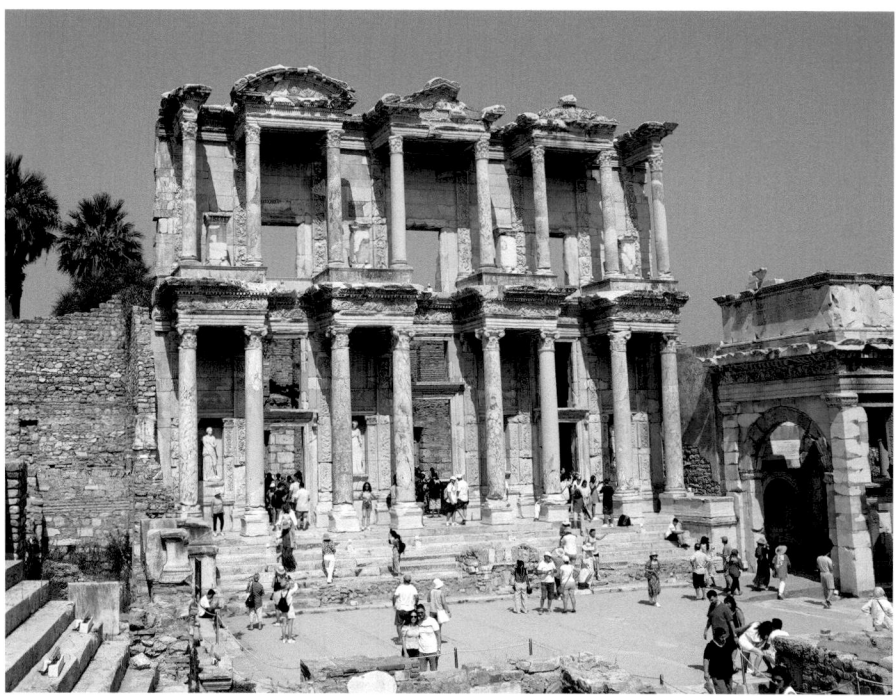

*Fig. 4. Library of Celsus,
Ephesus (photograph by the
author).*

of Tiberius Julius Celsus Polemaeanus, who served as proconsul of Asia and died around 112/113 C.E.[36] The building was begun by his son Tiberius Julius Aquila, whose own
premature death around 117 C.E. required the assistance of
another Ephesian benefactor, Tiberius Claudius Aristion, to
complete the construction.[37]

B. Burrell has described the library's external façade as having "no practical function whatsoever," because its two-story
exterior did not even correspond to the three-story interior
of the library space; in its sophisticated combination of aedicular architecture and statuary, the façade's overall design
was "so theatrical that it may have envisioned an audience
before it."[38] The façade's entrance was accessible via a staircase flanked by two bases for equestrian statues representing
Celsus. Four pairs of columns formed the front of the porch;
the entablature sprang forward over each pair, forming four
distyle aediculae. Within each aedicula was a wall niche carrying a statue of a personified virtue of Celsus standing on an
inscribed block.[39]

The intermedial games of this façade depend on the building's dual role as both a working library and a tomb of its
namesake, identified in a dedicatory inscription on the first-

story architraves.[40] Rather than declaring the recipient of the dedication in the dative, the inscription opens by naming the honoree (Celsus) in the accusative, in a manner evoking the epigraphic conventions of funerary statues.[41] Consequently, what is being announced as the object of dedication is not simply a library building or a tomb, but Celsus himself. As the first words of the inscription state, what Aquila dedicates is, in the accusative, Τι(βέριον) Ἰούλ[ιον Κέλσον Πολεμαιανὸν] ὕπατον ἀνθύπατον Ἀσίας ("Tiberius Julius Celsus Polemaeanus, consul and proconsul of Asia").

Both the equestrian statues and the four virtues were originally in bronze and are now lost. The four marble statues of draped women, found by the first-story niches at the time of excavation, are replacements added in late antiquity, probably at the moment when the dilapidated façade was transformed into a fountain.[42] As the indentations for metal tenons visible on the top surfaces of the equestrian bases demonstrate, the façade's original bronze statues were permanently affixed to their bases. Their subjects and positions are known through their surviving inscriptions. Any visitor to the library would first encounter two large statues of Celsus flanking the entrance stairs.[43] Each of the two bases has two separate texts: one on its short front side (letter height 4–6 cm), which recorded Celsus's name and his most important offices, and one on the inner, longer side, detailing a fuller *cursus honorum* (letter height 2–4 cm).[44] This difference in letter sizes was motivated not only by the length of the texts, but also by a dual address: larger letters faced viewers in the busy street, while smaller letters were appreciable by viewers who were already climbing the staircase.

While the letter heights on the equestrian bases are of a conventional height for statue bases, the identifying inscriptions below the four personified virtues in the niches of the first story are much larger (letter heights 8–11 cm). In fact, the size of the letters is more comparable to the dimensions of dedicatory inscriptions added to architraves of entire façades.[45] From left to right, they read Σοφία Κέλσου (Wisdom of Celsus),[46] Ἀρετὴ Κέλσου (Excellence of Celsus),[47] Ἔννοια Φιλίππου (Forethought of Philippos),[48] and Ἐπιστήμη Κέλσου (Knowledge of Celsus).[49] The bases for the four virtues are also unusual in their relationship to the façade. While the equestrian statues stood on stand-alone, profiled bases, which are separated from the wall of the façade

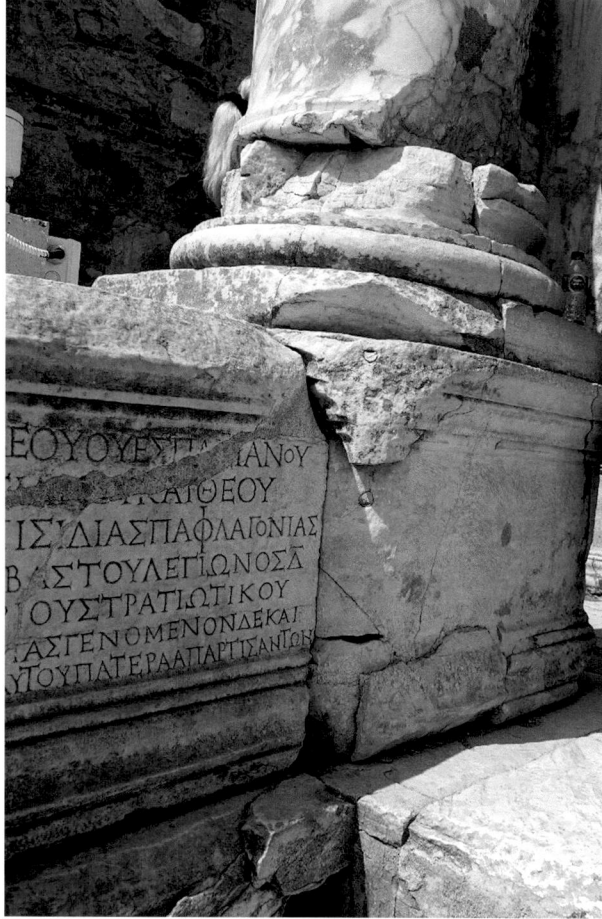

proper (fig. 5), the bases of the virtues are, in fact, only mock bases—they are embedded architectural blocks carved in relief to *look* like stand-alone profiled statue bases. Although the front of these blocks was carved to resemble the upper parts of statue bases (fig. 6), this was done in very shallow relief, and one could easily see the block extend all the way to the edges of the wall niche, leaving no gap visible (fig. 7).

With their feet affixed to blocks that were embedded into the niches in this manner, the bronze virtues of Celsus "belonged" structurally to the façade architecture. Their inscriptions enhance this play with the notion of belonging. As has been mentioned above, the dedicatory inscription for the whole building describes the object of dedication as being Celsus himself, in the accusative. Consequently, if the

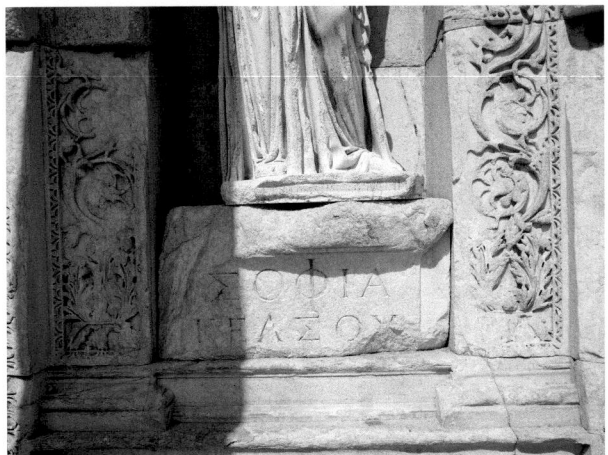

Fig. 6. Mock-statue base carved in shallow relief on the front surface of the block naming one of the virtues (photograph by the author).

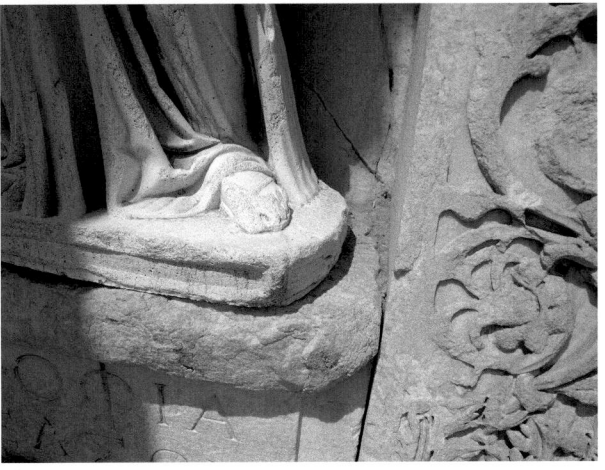

Fig. 7. Angled view of the same block, showing relationship between the inscribed surface and the niche (photograph by the author).

dedicated building *is* Celsus, then the four virtues are "of Celsus" in more than one way—the genitive Κέλσου can refer both to the man or the building.[50] The oversized lettering of their inscriptions, as well as their unusual identification using the nominative case, made the bronzes appear less like independent statues, and more like integral parts of the architecture.[51] By belonging to their façade in this way, the four virtues of Celsus play a role not unlike the one given to the pillar-backed figures in the Ephesus theater: the building to which the statues belonged took over some of their medial properties for its own purposes.

Conclusion

The two case studies from Ephesus introduce some of the methods for examining Roman attitudes toward the concept of medium, both in its artistic sense and as a social means of communication. They invite us to consider that Roman patrons had a sophisticated understanding not simply of *what* statues communicated to their audiences, but also *how* they did so, as mediated objects that interacted with other forms of material culture, such as architecture or inscriptions. By accentuating the status of statues as physical things, the façade dedications of Ephesian benefactors demonstrated an acute awareness of statues' medial properties. Playing with expectations of how statues ought to behave, these patrons helped visualize, in a more permanent way, the otherwise ephemeral performance of elevating a statue into its position.

The examples of the city's theater and the Library of Celsus illustrate the variety of approaches taken to accentuate medium-specific aspects of statuary, from the contrasting of the autonomy of in-the-round statues with pillar-backed statues, to the blurred use of epigraphic conventions of statue bases and building inscriptions. These case studies contribute to a broader understanding of Roman artistic practices, in which formal or noniconographic properties could be emphasized for rhetorical or aesthetic purposes.[52]

In Roman sculptural displays, the kind of medial play described above was by no means limited only to statuary on aedicular façades. However, unlike most statues in a Roman city, which were erected on the same horizontal plane used by their viewers, the façade statues occupied a kind of three-dimensional space—a stage—that humans could not access. By strategically blurring their own medial properties, these multimedia complexes dramatized the hierarchical relationships *between* their individual occupants—of which some were more autonomous than others. Fundamentally theatrical regardless of whether they appear in the context of a theater stage or on another kind of building, these statue-filled façades were a fruitful way for Romans to think through the relationships between objects, their dedicators, and their viewers.

Notes

¹ I would like to thank C. Marini and L. Tzortzopoulou-Gregory for inviting me to contribute to this volume. This chapter originated as the introduction of an AIA colloquium called *A Happy Medium: Media and Materiality in Ancient Art*, 6 January 2023. I would like to thank my co-organizer R. Pare, the colloquium presenters, and the anonymous readers for their feedback, in addition to R. Neer, J. Elsner, and G. Plattner.

² Ravasi 2015.

³ Berns 2002; Burrell 2006; Campagna 2018. These structures likely originate in the temporary wooden stages erected in Rome during the second and first centuries B.C.E. (Klar 2006).

⁴ Among the earliest are façades in Aphrodisias (28 B.C.E.) and Hierapolis (Augustan). Sobrà and Masino 2010, 374; 2014:175–76. In addition to theaters, they appear on public fountains (Dorl-Klingenschmid 2001, 48–53; Aristodemou 2011) and gateways (e.g., Strocka 1981), as well as in representative interior courtyards of bath-gymnasia (Burrell 2006).

⁵ As when Pliny disapprovingly mentions a Carthaginian statue of Hercules (*HN* 36.39), supposedly used for human sacrifices, as a work "without honor, and not in any temple" (*inhonorus est nec in templo ullo*); to make this lack of honor clearer, Pliny specifies that it can be seen "standing *on the ground*" (*humi stans*; emphasis added) in front of the Porticus ad Nationes in Rome, a reference best understood as signifying a lack of a pedestal. Many aspects of *damnatio memoriae* are similarly predicated on reading into the medium-specific relationship between a (now absent) statue and its (still present) base (Varner 2004).

⁶ Apul. *Flor.* 18; on the performance spaces of sophistic oratory, see Thomas 2017.

⁷ John Malalas, *Chron.* 9.11; Garstad 2005.

⁸ Schechtman 2020; see also Betancourt 2016.

⁹ Schechtman 2020, 68.

¹⁰ Quotation from Betancourt 2016, 164. This combination of theories is evidenced by Dietrich and Fouquet (2022), but also the approaches in Anguissola (2018) and Jones (2019).

¹¹ Zuiderhoek 2009.

¹² Stewart 2003, 92–108; Moormann 2008.

¹³ For more recent examples of remediation, or the representation of one medium in another, see the influential work of Bolter and Grusin (1999), productively applied by Jones (2019).

¹⁴ Stewart 2003, 92–108.

¹⁵ On aedicular framing mechanisms, see Platt and Squire 2017, 69–70.

¹⁶ On the reconstruction of the *scaenae frons*, see Öztürk 2010. On the theater, see Krinzinger and Ruggendorfer 2017, as well as

Heberdey et al. 1912; Sear 2006, 334–36; Gybas 2018, 16–30 (with earlier bibliography).

[17] *IvE* 2034; Krinzinger and Ruggendorfer 2017, 391–92, no. 2.

[18] A thorough reexamination of the finds, prepared by the author, may reveal specific campaigns of decoration. A brief survey of surviving statues was provided in Özren 1996, 107–8, 124–26.

[19] E.g., Vienna, Kunsthistorisches Museum I 932 (colossal head of Licinius).

[20] Vienna, Kunsthistorisches Museum I 1615 (Amazon), I 834 (satyr), I 1616 (Amazon), and I 1617 (unidentified); Eichler 1956; Hartswick 1986; Bol 1998, 193–94, nos. 2.12–13.

[21] Hartswick's (1986, 130 no. 3) identification of the figure as Dionysus is speculative.

[22] Bol 2011, 119, 121.

[23] Bol 1998, 193–94, following Eichler (1956, 10). An inscription from ca. 145 C.E. mentions the repair of the theater's προσκήνιον (*IvE* 2039).

[24] Cf. the 409 B.C.E. refurbishment inscription from the Athenian Erechtheion, in which the statues of the caryatids are referred to directly as *korai* (maidens; *IG* I³ 474).

[25] Embedded support figures of Dionysiac character—silenoi, satyrs, or maenads—are known from Hellenistic theaters in Sicily (Syracuse, Segesta, Iaitas; Schmidt 1982, 114–15). A large pillar-backed Silenus from the Dionysus theater in Athens may have provided a more immediate reference point. Sturgeon 1977, 48–50; Schmidt 1982, 123–25.

[26] Hölscher 2000, Langner 2014.

[27] On the motivations of façade patrons and their systems of reference, see Richard 2011, 86–93.

[28] Istanbul Archeological Museum 2454 (Aurenhammer 1990, 165–67, no. 146).

[29] *IvE* 2052. The seated figure is unlikely to be Demos, as it would be unprecedented to represent a bearded Demos in the nude (Aurenhammer 1990, 167).

[30] *RPC* II, 1073 (Domitian); III, 2058–59 (Hadrian); VI, 4861 (Elagabalus); VI, 4965 (Severus Alexander). Despite affinities with the Pheidian Zeus of Olympia, the Zeus on Ephesian coins is distinguished by his uncovered genitals—one of the more unusual aspects of the seated marble statue as well. The earliest appearance of this Zeus type on coins is in the reign of Domitian, the same emperor to whom the Ephesian stage façade was dedicated (*RPC* II, 1073). If the marble statue once held a statuette of Artemis of Ephesus, to whom the stage was also dedicated, its inclusion in the center of the Domitianic stage would be even more fitting.

[31] E.g., Mart. *Spect.* 2.2.

[32] In Aphrodisias, several statues set up on the stage are explicitly identified as restored and repaired objects (e.g., *IAph* 8.86). In Miletus, the Late Archaic torso of Apollo belonged to an ancient statue

whose repair and redisplay in the theater was politically motivated (Bol 2005).

[33] Aurenhammer 1990, 165–67.

[34] *IvE* 2039.

[35] Wilberg et al. 1953; Hueber and Strocka 1975; Strocka 1978, 2009; Burrell 2009, 78–82; Portale 2011; Graham 2013, 398–402.

[36] *IvE* 5113. Strocka 2009, 247.

[37] *IvE* 5101. Strocka 1978, 898.

[38] Burrell 2009, 82.

[39] Wilberg et al. 1953, 3–4, fig. 4.

[40] *IvE* 5101. Graham (2013, 398–401) discusses the distribution of text across the blocks of the first story architraves.

[41] Burrell 2009, 78; Portale 2011, 118–19.

[42] Eichler 1953; on the transformation, see Thür 2020.

[43] Keil 1953, 62–66, 73–74; Burrell 2009, 80–81; Strocka 2009, 247; Graham 2013, 400–1.

[44] *IvE* 5102–3.

[45] The library's dedicatory inscription has a letter height of 9.5 cm (Graham 2013, 398).

[46] *IvE* 5108; letter height 9 cm (l. 1), 7.5 cm (l. 2).

[47] *IvE* 5109; letter height 11 cm.

[48] *IvE* 5110; letter height 8 cm. The base's inscription is a Late Antique replacement: the original incised inscription was replaced with one painted in red paint. Originally, it too must have been a virtue of Celsus (Keil 1953, 72).

[49] *IvE* 5111; letter height 8.5 cm (l. 1), 7 cm (l. 2).

[50] That statues in a façade belonged to it is also suggested by the dedicatory inscription of Zoilos's theater in Aphrodisias (28 B.C.E.), which refers to "the proskenion with all the ornaments *in it*" (τὸ προσκήν[ι]ον σὺν τοῖς ἐν αὐ[τῶι π]ροσκοσμήμασιν πᾶσιν, *IAph* 8.1, 8.5). See also *IK Side* II 140. The author is currently preparing a more comprehensive study of such inscriptions, which will clarify how the relationship between the façade and its statues was perceived.

[51] Cf. *IK Perge* I 101–109.

[52] E.g., Hölscher 2004.

Works Cited

Anguissola, A. 2018. *Supports in Roman Marble Sculpture: Workshop Practice and Modes of Viewing*. Cambridge: Cambridge University Press.

Aristodemou, G. 2011. "Theatre Façades and Façade Nymphaea: The Link between." *BCH* 135:163–97. DOI: 10.3406/bch.2011.7831.

Aurenhammer, M. 1990. *Die Skulpturen von Ephesos: Bildwerke Aus Stein*. Ephesos 10.1. Vienna: Verlag der Österreichischen Akademie der Wissenschaften.

Berns, C. 2002. "Frühkaiserzeitliche Tabernakelfassaden: Zum Beginn eines Leitmotivs urbaner Architektur in Kleinasien." In *Patris und Imperium: Kulturelle und politische Identität in den Städten der römischen Provinzen Kleinasiens in der frühen Kaiserzeit; Kolloquium Köln, November 1998*, edited by C. Berns, H. von Hesberg, L. Vandeput, and M. Waelkens, 159–74. BABESCH Suppl. 8. Leuven: Peeters.

Betancourt, R. 2016. "Introduction: The Medium before Modernism." *West 86th* 23:163–67.

Bol, R. 1998. *Amazones Volneratae: Untersuchungen zu den Ephesischen Amazonenstatuen.* Mainz: Philipp von Zabern.

———. 2005. "Der Torso von Milet und die Statue des Apollon Termintheus in Myus." *IstMitt* 55:37–64.

———. 2011. *Funde aus Milet, Teil 2: Marmorskulpturen der römischen Kaiserzeit aus Milet.* Milet 5.2. Berlin: Walter de Gruyter.

Bolter, J.D., and R.A. Grusin. 1999. *Remediation: Understanding New Media.* Cambridge: MIT Press.

Burrell, B. 2006. "False Fronts: Separating the Aedicular Façade from the Imperial Cult in Roman Asia Minor." *AJA* 110:437–69. DOI: 10.3764/aja.110.3.437.

Burrell, B. 2009. "Reading, Hearing, and Looking at Ephesos." In *Ancient Literacies: The Culture of Reading in Greece and Rome*, edited by W.A. Johnson and H.N. Parker, 69–95. Oxford: Oxford University Press.

Campagna, L. 2018. "I ninfei di Hierapolis e l'architettura delle fontane monumentali di età romana in Asia Minore." In *Hierapolis di Frigia. XI: Il Ninfeo dei Tritoni*, edited by L. Campagna, 599–634. Istanbul: Ege Yayınları.

Dietrich, N., and J. Fouquet, eds. 2022. *Image, Text, Stone: Intermedial Perspectives on Graeco-Roman Sculpture.* Materiale Textkulturen 36. Berlin: Walter de Gruyter.

Dorl-Klingenschmid, C. 2001. *Prunkbrunnen in Kleinasiatischen Städten: Funktion Im Kontext.* Studien zur antiken Stadt 7. Munich: Dr. Friedrich Pfeil.

Eichler, F. 1953. "Die Skulpturen." In *Die Bibliothek*, edited by W. Wilberg, M. Theuer, F. Eichler, and J. Keil, 47–60. Ephesos 5.1. Vienna: Österreichisches Archäologisches Institut.

———. 1956. "Eine neue Amazone und andere Skulpturen aus dem Theater von Ephesos." *ÖJh* 43:7–18.

Garstad, B. 2005. "The Tyche Sacrifices in John Malalas: Virgin Sacrifice and Fourth-Century Polemical History." *Illinois Classical Studies* 30:83–135.

Graham, A.S. 2013. "The Word Is Not Enough: A New Approach to Assessing Monumental Inscriptions; A Case Study from Roman Ephesos." *AJA* 117:383–412. DOI: 10.3764/aja.117.3.0383.

Gybas, M. 2018. *Das Theater in der Stadt und die Stadt im Theater:*

Urbanistischer Kontext und Funktionen von Theatern im kaiserzeitlichen Kleinasien. Antiquitates 69. Hamburg: Verlag Dr. Kovač.

Hartswick, K.J. 1986. "The So-Called Ephesos Amazon: A New Identification." *JdI* 101:126–36.

Heberdey, R., G. Niemann, and W. Wilberg, eds. 1912. *Das Theater in Ephesos.* Ephesos 2. Vienna: Alfred Hölder.

Hölscher, T. 2000. "Die Amazonen von Ephesos: Ein Monument der Selbstbehauptung." In *Agathos daimon: Mythes et cultes; Études d'iconographie en l'honneur de Lilly Kahil,* edited by P. Linant de Bellefonds, 205–18. BCH Suppl. 38. Paris: École Française d'Athènes.

———. 2004. *The Language of Images in Roman Art.* Cambridge: Cambridge University Press.

Hueber, F., and V.M. Strocka. 1975. "Die Bibliothek des Celsus: Eine Prachtfassade in Ephesos und das Problem ihrer Wiederaufrichtung." *AntW* 6, no. 4:3–14.

Jones, N.B. 2019. *Painting, Ethics, and Aesthetics in Rome.* Greek Culture in the Roman World. Cambridge: Cambridge University Press.

Keil, J. 1953. "Die Inschriften." In *Die Bibliothek,* edited by W. Wilberg, M. Theuer, F. Eichler and J. Keil, 61–80. Ephesos 5.1. Vienna: Österreichisches Archäologisches Institut.

Klar, L.S. 2006. "The Origins of the Roman *Scaenae Frons* and the Architecture of Triumphal Games in the Second Century B.C." In *Representations of War in Ancient Rome,* edited by S. Dillon and K. Welch, 162–83. Cambridge: Cambridge University Press.

Krinzinger, F., and P. Ruggendorfer, eds. 2017. *Das Theater von Ephesos: Archäologischer Befund, Funde und Chronologie.* Ephesos 2.1. Vienna: Verlag der Österreichischen Akademie der Wissenschaften. DOI: 10.2307/j.ctv8d5sk4.

Langner, M. 2014. "Amazonen als Einwanderer. Ursprung, Konstruktion und Dekonstruktion mythischer Verwandtschaft in Athen und Ephesos." In *Genealogie und Migrationsmythen im antiken Mittelmeerraum und auf der arabischen Halbinsel,* edited by A.-B. Renger and I. Toral-Niehoff, 105–36. Berlin: Edition Topoi.

Moormann, E.M. 2008. "Statues on the Wall: The Representation of Statuary in Roman Wall Painting." In *The Sculptural Environment of the Roman Near East,* edited by Y.Z. Eliav, E.A. Friedland, and S. Herbert, 197–224. Interdisciplinary Studies in Ancient Culture and Religion 9. Leuven: Peeters.

Özren, A.C. 1996. "Die Skulpturenausstattung kaiserzeitlicher Theater in der Provinz Asia, am Beispiel der Theater in Aphrodisias, Ephesos und Hierapolis." *Thetis* 3:99–128.

Öztürk, A. 2010. "Das Bühnengebäude und seine flavische Scaenae Frons des Theaters in Ephesos." In *La scaenae frons en la* arquitectura teatral romana: Actas del symposium internacional celebrado en Cartagena los días 12 al 14 de marzo de 2009 en el Museo del Teatro Romano, edited by S.F. Ramallo Asensio and N. Röring, 331–42. Murcia: Universidad de Murcia.

Platt, V.J., and M. Squire, eds. 2017. The Frame in Classical Art: A Cultural History. Cambridge: Cambridge University Press.

Portale, E.C. 2011. "Ancora sulla Kelsiane Bibliotheke di Efeso." Mediterraneo antico 14, no. 1/2:107–48.

Ravasi, T. 2015. "Displaying Sculpture in Rome." In A Companion to Ancient Aesthetics, edited by P. Destrée and P. Murray, 248–61. Hoboken: John Wiley & Sons. DOI: 10.1002/9781119009795.ch16.

Richard, J. 2011. "In the Elites' Toolkit: Decoding the Initiative and Reference System behind the Investment in the Architecture and Decoration of Roman Nymphaea." Facta 5:65–100.

Schechtman, A. 2020. "The Medium Concept." Representations 150:61–90. DOI: 10.1525/rep.2020.150.1.61.

Schmidt, E. 1982. Geschichte der Karyatide: Funktion und Bedeutung der menschlichen Träger- und Stützfigur in der Baukunst. Beitrage zur Archäologie 13. Würzburg: Konrad Triltsch Verlag.

Sear, F. 2006. Roman Theatres: An Architectural Study. Oxford Monographs on Classical Archaeology. Oxford; New York: Oxford University Press.

Sobrà, G., and F. Masino. 2010. "La frontescena severiana del teatro di Hierapolis di Frigia: Architettura, decorazione e maestranza." In La scaenae frons en la arquitectura teatral romana, edited by S.F. Ramallo Asensio and N. Röring, 373–412. Murcia: Universidad de Murcia.

———. 2014. "Theatre Buildings of the Early Imperial Age in Asia Minor: Some Dating Elements." In Akti XII. Međunarodnog Kolokvija o Rimskoj Provincijalnoj Umjetnosti, 173–76. Pula: Arheološki muzej Istre.

Stewart, P. 2003. Statues in Roman Society: Representation and Response. Oxford Studies in Ancient Culture and Representation. Oxford: Oxford University Press.

Strocka, V.M. 1978. "Zur Datierung der Celsusbibliothek." In Proceedings of the Xth International Congress of Classical Archaeology Ankara-Izmir 1973, edited by E. Akurgal, 893–900. Ankara: Türk Tarih Kurumu.

———. 1981. Das Markttor von Milet. Winckelmannsprogramm der Archäologischen Gesellschaft zu Berlin 128. Berlin: Walter de Gruyter.

———. 2009. "Die Celsusbibliothek als Ehrengrab am Embolos." In Neue Forschungen zur Kuretenstraße von Ephesos, edited by S. Ladstätter, 247–59. Archäologische Forschungen 15. Vienna: Verlag der Österreichischen Akademie der Wissenschaften.

Sturgeon, M.C. 1977. "The Reliefs on the Theater of Dionysos in Athens." *AJA* 81:31–53. DOI: 10.2307/503646.

Thomas, E. 2017. "Performance Space." In *The Oxford Handbook to the Second Sophistic*, edited by D.A. Richter and W.A. Johnson, 181–202. Oxford: Oxford University Press.

Thür, H. 2020. "Von der Bibliothek zum Brunnen: Umnutzung und Umbau in hydrotechnischem Kontext. Ein Bauprogramm im spätantiken Ephesos?" In *Umgebaut: Umbau-, Umnutzungs- und Umwertungsprozesses in der antiken Architektur*, edited by U. Wulf-Rheidt and K. Piesker, 333–48. Diskussionen zur archäologischen Bauforschung 13. Regensburg: Schnell & Steiner.

Varner, E. 2004. *Mutilation and Transformation: Damnatio Memoriae and Roman Imperial Portraiture*. Monumenta Graeca et Romana 10. Leiden: Brill.

Wilberg, W., M. Theuer, F. Eichler, and J. Keil. 1953. *Die Bibliothek*. Ephesos 5.1. Vienna: Österreichisches Archäologisches Institut.

Zuiderhoek, A. 2009. *The Politics of Munificence in the Roman Empire: Citizens, Elites and Benefactors in Asia Minor*. Greek Culture in the Roman World. Cambridge: Cambridge University Press.

Containing Yourself: Romano-British Face Pots as Proxy for Body and Self

Danielle Vander Horst

Abstract

This study seeks to offer a new approach to Romano-British face pots wherein these vessels can be understood as active agents in sociocultural contexts related to votive and funerary practices. First, I will briefly define the vessels at hand before looking to anthropological theory in order to help frame how such vessels were able to act in embodied ways within Romano-British contexts. I will then take these anthropological approaches and apply them to ideas about the human body in Iron Age Britain in order to understand key demographic variances between consumers of Romano-British face pots and consumers of their counterparts in the continental empire. The result of this discussion is that face pots in Britain may be seen as productive outlets for pre-Roman ideologies concerning what the body is and how it can look and how, as proxies for human agents, they can act as agents in their own right.

Introduction

ROMAN FACE POTS ARE A WIDELY DISTRIBUTED, ALBEIT statistically uncommon, ceramic type with recorded finds across the provinces of Hispania, Germania, Gaul, Britannia, Italia, Pannonia, Dacia, and Moesia. They vary in size, but overall are globular in shape and have a face on the body of the vessel (fig. 1).[1] The bodies of these vessels are wheel-made in local fabrics while the faces are shaped and applied by hand after the pot has been formed. Thus, there are no two identical face pots even when produced by the same potter.

While Roman face pots are not a material phenomenon unique to Britain, those found within Britannia display iconographic and consumption-based distributional differences distinct enough from the rest of the Roman face-pot corpus as to warrant a need for new perspectives and research questions regarding who made them, how they were used,

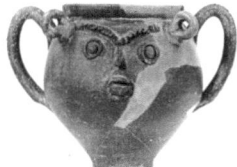

IT Type 4 from Viterbo. h: 9 cm

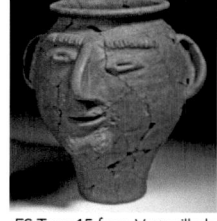

FS Type 15 from Vatteville-la-Rue, h: 17.6 cm

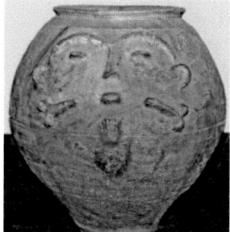

RD Type 11 from Bad-Cannstatt, h: 35 cm

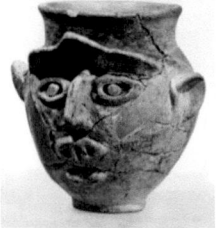

DAN Type 13 from Intercisa, h: 12.5 cm

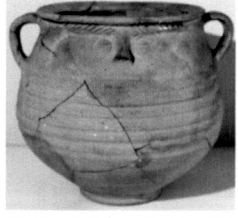

RB Type 13E from East Studdale, h: 19.7 cm

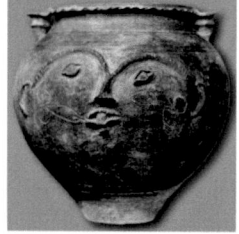

RL Type 2B from Köln, h: 29.3 cm

Fig. 1. Roman face pots with features characteristic of their respective regions (after Braithwaite 2007).

by whom, and to what ends. The result of this inquiry is a novel approach to Romano-British face pots wherein we may utilize anthropological frameworks in new ways to continue to expand our understanding of provincial identities through the purposeful consumption and deposition of foreign materials for local purposes.[2] More specifically, through these vessels, I argue that it is possible to discern the persistence of Late pre-Roman Iron Age ideologies surrounding the body and embodied object agency within a rapidly changing social landscape.

Active Vessels and Containers

This inquiry is, at its core, concerned with how certain peoples—Romano-Britons—understood vessels to be multifaceted objects capable of engaging in cultural practices as embodied, active agents. Of course, object agency is, in and of itself, a topic that has generated ample debate on the full extent of its applicability, however, for the sake of this study, we will assume an approach that understands material culture as comprising intentionally created objects imbued with social purposes that they aim to fulfill through action, thus obtaining agency.[3] It then follows that objects' associated meanings and capacity for agency must be understood as contextually derived from as well as dependent upon their unique material and iconographic-based affordances.[4] For example, a ceramic

126

vessel will be a more or less effective agent in certain tasks and practices than, say, an iron axe or a wooden chair. If the goal is to provide a location of containment, about which we are concerned here, the vessel will prove most effective. C. Knappet and colleagues considered this issue of ceramic containers and asserted the importance of distinguishing *ceramic container* as a unique category within material studies precisely for their particular ability of containment that, they argued, mimics the containing capabilities of the human body, a container for the self.[5] If we add to their work J.-P. Warnier's approach to socially embedded ceramic vessels we can see even more clearly the cognitive metaphor at play in replacing human bodies with ceramic containers.[6]

Warnier bases his work on Mausian concepts of *technique du corps*, in which material engagements are dependent upon the physical sensibilities and capabilities of the human body, but what Warnier adds to M. Maus's thesis is that our physical conducts with regards to objects require corresponding drive and emotions. This he terms "sensori-affectivo-motor-conducts geared toward material culture."[7] In looking at ceramic vessels, Warnier proposes that bodies and vessels are closely linked, suggesting that the skin and the clay afford the same acts of containment that Knappett and colleagues discuss, providing loci in which techniques of the self are formed and performed.[8] Just as we care for our skin, a vessel's surface is treated with great care, often decorated, glazed, or smoothed. The reasoning for doing so, Warnier argues, is (1) because certain surface treatments add a layer of protection or adornment to the vessel, and (2) because in altering the exterior of the vessel one is able to "enhance the emotional dimension of its sensori-motor manipulation," granting it a style that acts as a means of both external identification and iconography-induced satisfaction not dissimilar to personal acts of adornment and grooming.[9] Face pots then, as ceramic vessels, share the containment possibilities that Knappet and colleagues argue for, and the detailed care taken in forming their faces, by Warnier's reasoning, adds greatly to the "emotional dimensions" of their desirability as human media.[10]

Anthropomorphic containers with faces extend the metaphor of vessel to body, body to vessel even further through processes of communicative signaling by way of facial imagery. H. Belting's definition of images as being more than simply "product[s] of perception" but as things that are created out of personal or collective knowledge bases is particularly applicable here.[11] Face pots can be read not just as aesthetic choices but as potent cultural symbols that are socially embedded and based on collective consensus of what an image can be and what it can do. Belting further reckons that ontologies of and reactions to imagery are not universal and are instead relational and contextually derived. Thus, while we can understand that having a human body is a universal experience, the ways in which it is both experienced and conceptualized are not.[12] By this reasoning, how the body can be translated to alternative media, through what materials and to what ends, can differ between and within groups.

With the face as our image, we can also consider E. Goffman's important work on communicative potential through iconographic signaling, allowing us to fully see the face pots with their combined material and facial iconography as social agents in their own right able to serve as loci for human identities and as replacements for human agents.[13] Goffman asserts that the basic features that make up the human face and make us capable of effective communication as agents are the eyes, mouth, ears, nose, and the expressive addition of eyebrows. This visage, he says, is the image through which we are known by other social agents and how we produce a socially engaged self that can participate in the rituals demanded by our societal contexts. Therefore, according to Goffman, facial media are critical aspects of what grant us agency within social rituals and circumstances.

Coalescing these ideas and applying them to materials that utilize the same facial media that allow human agents to act as social agents—that is, the face pots—I propose that Roman face pots may take on human-like capabilities of agency and engagement. Warnier's and Knappet and colleague's logic allows us to view the face pots' ceramic material and purposefully constructed form as potential loci in which the human identity can be performed and contained, while from Goffman's perspective we can view the facial media of the face pots (their ears, noses, mouths, eyes, and eyebrows) as the means through which they act as agents in their own right, even becoming human proxies for social practices when engaged with in certain circumstances.[14]

Now, this is not to say that every face pot in Roman Britain was meant to be engaged with as such or that every face pot acted as a human proxy, but I would argue that the combination of their media and materiality *within certain charged contexts* may point toward behaviors and consumption patterns possibly marked by local and/or pre-Roman preferences and beliefs regarding the human body and identity.

Britain and Iron Age Bodies

Prior to the Roman conquest, anthropomorphic art was sparse in Britain, but this should certainly not be understood as a lack of access to techniques or knowledge on how to reproduce such images.[15] Recent decades of work have demonstrated that Britain was not an island in isolation during the Iron Age but was actively engaged in trading networks with the continent and beyond.[16] J.D. Hill and C. Gosden have both shown, however, that imported art and iconographic pieces were few and far between and they have argued persuasively for a uniquely British tradition of artistic objects crafted on the island that sparingly created the full human body but did produce the human head in various ways.[17]

The work of I. Armit has illustrated how thoroughly entrenched ideas and practices related to the human head were in Celtic cultures during the Iron Age through a large-scale analysis of iconography and ritualistic deposits of human crania and cranial media.[18] He concluded that the head was a potent icon of power and identity, often spurring traditions of headhunting and trophy display in conflicts between tribes, and he showed that crania and cranial media in particular served in many ways as focal points of religious and funerary practices with ample evidence of foundational and votive shaft, well, and river basin deposits across Britain and much of northern Europe. While he does argue that the evidence does not go so far as to indicate a universal cult of the head, he does contend that crania and images of heads/faces held particular symbolic and emotional value for Iron Age peoples as a means of apotropaic protection and, most importantly, as primary focal points of identity formation, display, and performance.[19] Considering the importance and pervasiveness of such images, it is unreasonable to assume that practices involving facial/cranial iconography would simply vanish under Roman rule.

While older paradigms of Roman provincial studies might have argued that with the onset of conquest also dawned the inevitable replacement of local cultures with more Roman styles of living, more modern scholarly inquiries have taken postcolonial approaches to narrative construction that grant equal space for local cultures to both exert autonomy in culture creation and impact those who conquer just as much they are impacted as the conquered.[20] Persistent cultural memories applied and engaged through new media and cultural methods have been one result of such studies. Analyses of Romano-Celtic and Romano-Gallic temples as well as ritual behaviors in Britain have produced much fruitful dialogue, and, pertinent to our purposes here, M. Aldhouse-Green has highlighted how the southeast of Britain in particular has proven a hotbed for examples of "independence from Classical symbolism" in the construction and utilization of mixed cultural material.[21] Such independence and resistance to all-consuming change can occur through stylistic variations of imported objects/structures or local practices making use of foreign materials. We can observe a similar phenomenon with Roman face pots in Britain wherein newly introduced media and material combinations are found to be applicable to pre-existing local ideologies and contribute to the persistence and continued practice of preconquest belief systems.

British Face Pot Distributions and Types

In this way, it must always be understood that within British contexts, face pots are Roman products introduced by the Roman military during the invasion of 43 C.E.; there are no examples of Roman face pots in Britain prior to this event. G. Braithwaite's seminal studies of the vessels have concluded two important points to this end: one, empire-wide face pot distribution is predominately focused around Roman military communities (forts and *vici*); and two, they are most commonly recovered from burial contexts as cinerary urns, followed by general domestic contexts without definitively ascribed functions.[22] Braithwaite argues that the face pots were likely chthonic or apotropaic in nature, not meant to replicate or represent any living or deceased individual but anthropomorphic, divine entities.[23] Furthermore, continental pots (fig.1) often display rather exaggerated and dramatic features (elongated and hooked noses, protruding ears, horns, etc.) that extend beyond simple abstraction into the realm of nonhuman.[24]

In the early conquest period of Britain, face pots occurred in areas with an active military presence (fig. 2), as might be expected based on continental patterns. By the mid- to late-

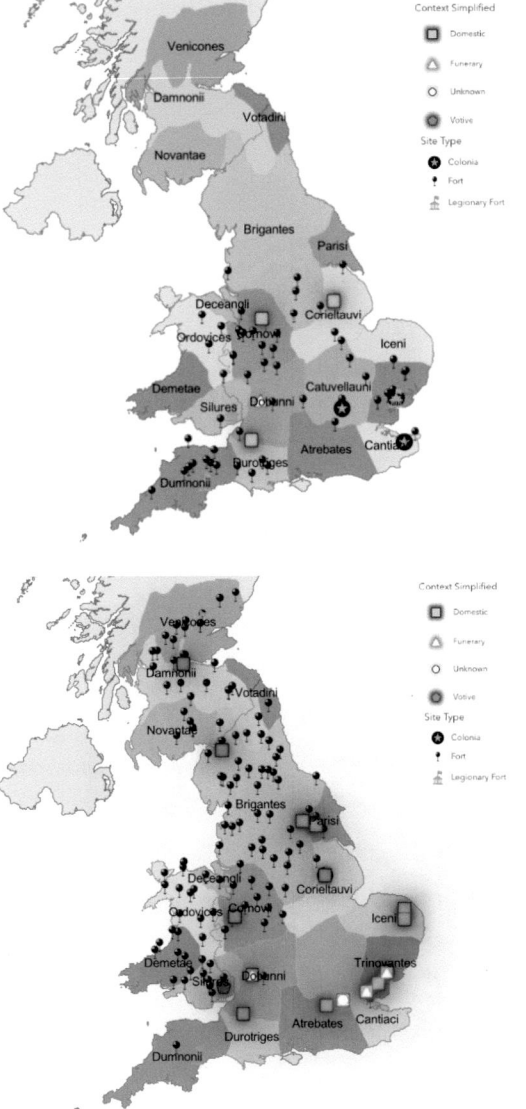

Fig. 2. Face pot distribution by site and context type during the Julio-Claudian phase, 43–ca. 68 C.E. Map chronology based on movement of military and fort statuses after Jones and Mattingly 2007. Face pots represented here are based on presence of types, not quantity.

Fig. 3. Face pot distribution by site and context type during the Flavian phase, ca. 69–96 C.E. Map chronology based on movement of military and fort statuses after Jones and Mattingly 2007. Face pots represented here are based on presence of types, not quantity.

first-century C.E., however, face pots are found in much higher numbers in southeast England where active military forts are decreasing in number and where the so-called civilian zone was beginning to develop (fig. 3).[25] Furthermore, figures 4 and 5 demonstrate that, between these two periods and beyond into the early third-century C.E., the number of military funerary uses of the vessels decreases significantly, while votive uses among military populations disappear entirely.[26]

131

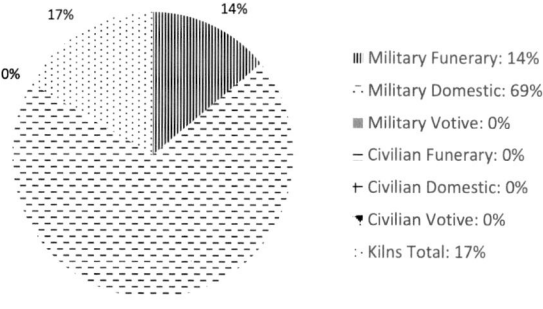

Fig. 4. Face pot distribution ratios by site type (military or civilian) and by context (domestic, votive, funerary, kilns) between 43 C.E. and ca. 85 C.E. Chronology after Braithwaite 2007. N = 36 minimum number of individuals.

Initial Conquest Phase (43 - ca. 85 CE)

ıⅡ Military Funerary: 14%
⁝⸫ Military Domestic: 69%
■ Military Votive: 0%
— Civilian Funerary: 0%
+ Civilian Domestic: 0%
▼ Civilian Votive: 0%
⸬⸫ Kilns Total: 17%

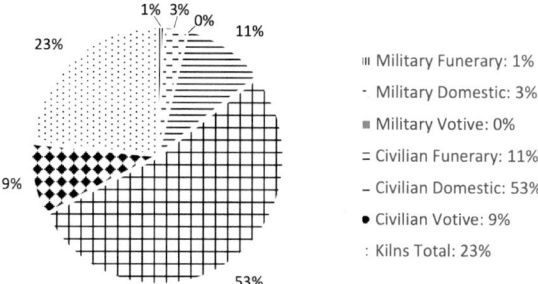

Fig. 5. Face pot distribution ratios by site type (military or civilian) and by context (domestic, votive, funerary, kilns) between ca. 85 C.E. and 225 C.E. Chronology after Braithwaite 2007. N = 132 minimum number of individuals.

Northern Expansion and Provincial Phase (ca. 85 - ca. 225 CE)

ıⅡ Military Funerary: 1%
⁻ Military Domestic: 3%
■ Military Votive: 0%
= Civilian Funerary: 11%
– Civilian Domestic: 53%
● Civilian Votive: 9%
⁚ Kilns Total: 23%

On the civilian side, both funerary and votive uses of these vessels increase considerably by the mid-second-century C.E. As a whole, between the conquest (43 C.E.) and up through the Hadriannic period and beyond (ca. 138–225 C.E.), the overwhelming majority of face pots occur in the southeastern portions of the province (fig. 6).[27]

Aside from geographic proximity and social/economic familiarity with Rome preconquest in the southeast of Britain, one reason that may contribute to the consumption pattern differences observed in British face pots is their particular set of facial characteristics that set them apart from continental examples.[28] Figure 7 shows a selection of face pots emblematic of the Romano-British variation, which are known for their languid, somber expressions with small eyes and often closed mouths. Though by no means anatomically accurate or realistic, these faces give a closer impression of a human face (or at

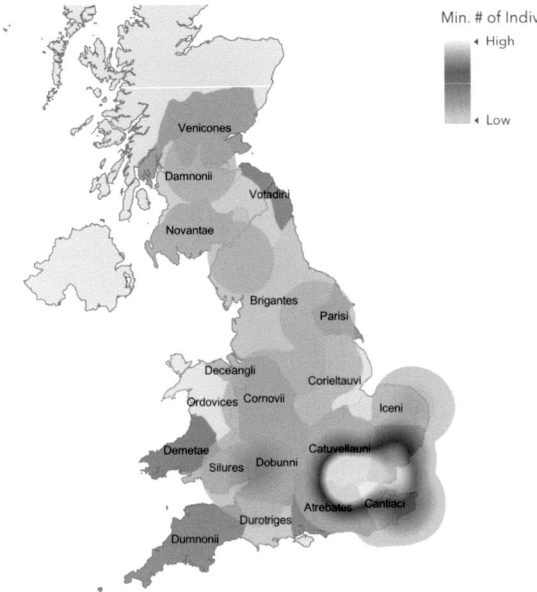

Min. # of Indiv.

◄ High

◄ Low

Fig. 6. Heatmap distribution of all face pot finds in England between 43 C.E. and ca. 138 C.E. The highest concentration of vessels can be found in the southeast of England in regions previously inhabited by the Atrebates, Catuvellauni, Trinovantes, and Cantiaci tribes. N = 170 minimum number of individuals.

least the schema of one) compared to the exaggerated expressions and features of the continental pots (fig. 1) and would seem to adhere to the preference among Iron Age Britons for abstraction of the human form.[29] As such, most Romano-British vessels make use of the so-called sliced mushroom nose and eyebrow combination, and coffee-bean or mound-like eyes. Mouths are often simply slits or depressions in the clay, and ears are either fashioned separately and applied to the surface or incised as upside-down fishhook shapes. Chins are applied as small mounds or are absent entirely. Overall, the faces of these vessels share striking similarities with the faces of Iron Age Europe, furthering their appeal to Celtic ideals.[30]

What's more, the Romano-British vessels also exhibit a certain level of what I would argue is gender-neutrality in that they do not appear to be exclusively associated with any one gender in terms of either their iconography or accompanying markers in burial contexts.[31] The faces, too, lack much in the way of overly individualized or gendered features, typically constructing facial expressions from generic and formulaic shapes.[32] While some vessels do possess beards, features which can be indicative of a more masculine identity, they are not a statistically standard feature for the face pot corpus as a whole.

133

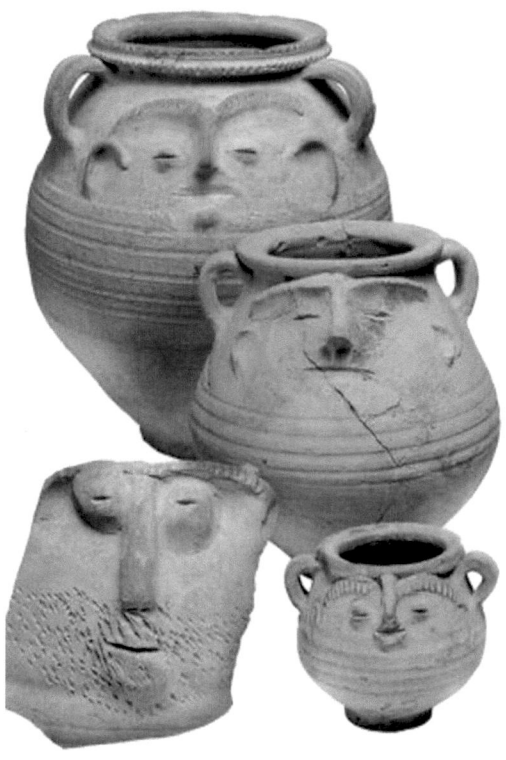

By description alone, it may seem that the pots were subject to a certain level of homogeneity, yet it is clear from the examples in figure 7 that even within this repertoire of forms and features each pot still presented a unique combination of style and expression while maintaining their basic human qualities, unlike many examples from the European continent. The reasoning for this preference for a simpler yet clearly recognizable human construction of the face may be understood as being in communication with the preceding Iron Age traditions of the body and preferences for schematized, abstract formulations of the face when creating anthropomorphic media and their ability to represent living or deceased individuals. For this reason, the face pots utilized in religious contexts are of particular note.[33]

Face pots from funerary contexts offer the most obvious means of exploring the ideas above in their use as cinerary urns. In these contexts, face pots have exchanged flesh and blood faces—or Goffmanian human agents—with ceramic ones and, as representations of that which has been lost or is gone, they are engaged with as symbolic replacements for the perishable and transient human body, offering a new vessel in which the identity of an individual may persist into death.[34] Of course, we must acknowledge that most burial contexts are constructed by those who have survived the deceased rather than the deceased themselves, yet despite this, ontological perspectives were still at play wherein the ceramic face pot was seen as a productive, materialistic replacement for the media and physicality of the human body in which identity was formed.[35]

If we also foreground that the head in particular held emotional and symbolic value for Iron Age peoples, the face pots, as new representations of those images, could also be interpreted as presenting an additional realm of material value, occupying the middle-zone between the three factors that L. Büster argues are critical to consider when looking at materials chosen for purposeful deposition: material value, symbolic value, and emotional value.[36]

Furthermore, the replication of the human form in socio-culturally charged contexts through mimetic media is not a new phenomenon and we can see similar substitutions across many cultural traditions. The canopic urns of Etruria are a prime example. Traditional Etruscan style urns such as those from Chiusi were certainly meant to replicate and replace the human body, however, when new media became available and images of the face and body shifted to more hellenized forms, the altered appearance of the urn enabled a new level of material agency for the vessel through its new media.[37] Face pots in funerary and other religious contexts exhibit much the same behavior, allowing for new material and media-based expressions of cultural practices with enhanced levels of engagement lent to material agents by virtue of their combined characteristics and ontological beliefs related to the human body.[38]

Case Studies from London and Verulamium

Taking what we have established above, let us consider two face pot from Britain in context. Since connections between bodies and ceramic urns have been well established, I wish to focus here on votive vessels as proxies for human agents and human bodies: a mid-second-century-C.E. vessel from the London Walbrook Stream site in the old River Thames

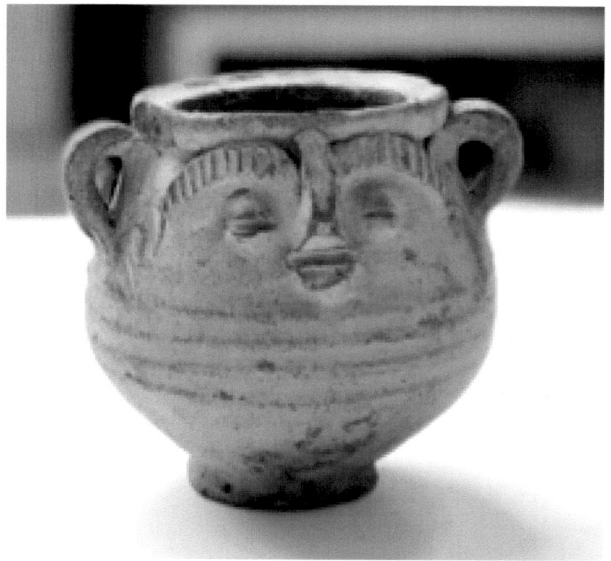

Fig. 8. A mid-second century C.E. face pot from Walbrook Stream, London. Museum of London, A1739, height: 11.6 cm (photograph by author, by permission of the Museum of London).

basin (fig. 8) and a mid-second to third-century-C.E. face pot deposited within a votive shaft in Roman Verulamium.

While it had previously been thought that the Walbrook streambed served as nothing more than a site for residential rubbish refuse, later work demonstrated that it was in fact an area rife with ritual behaviors, many of which showed strong connections to pre-Roman practices.[39] At least 100 human crania were located across this area, many in purposeful depositional contexts, as were multiple face pots.[40] While connections to the cemetery further along the stream are still murky, the ritually charged aspects of these cranial and ceramic deposits and their relation to Iron Age practices have found no opposition.[41] It has been remarked upon that the ceramic face pots in this area were engaged in similar if not entirely substitutive practices for Iron Age traditions, mirroring the deposition of human skulls.[42] Such claims are further substantiated by the relative ages of these objects, with the majority of the skulls dating to the Iron Age and early Roman period and the face pots dating well into the late-first and mid-second century.[43] If Iron Age practices involving genuine human remains were being adapted to suit a more Roman-controlled social climate, then a substitution for objects that offered comparable media and material characteristics is not unreasonable if the new objects in question still allowed for cultural practices to be carried out in similarly emotionally charged manners. Of course, we cannot definitively ascribe the use of any one of the face pots found to any one individual of particular cultural or ethnic backgrounds, but it is meaningful that such an item—one of Roman origin—was seemingly being utilized in a context that speaks to pre-Roman religious practices in a setting with significant Iron Age connotations (i.e., a waterscape).[44] The vessel in figure 8 very well could have served in this or other proxy functions for living individuals at a shrine or other religious structures further upstream in the cemetery. Beyond the obvious objectified substitution for a human skull, it also possesses all of the necessary features and characteristics according to Warnier, Goffman, and Belting to replicate the active agency of a human worshiper in communication with deities.[45] The face of the pot presents a human focal point for the attention of the god while also potentially serving as a vessel in more literal terms for offerings. Communicative connection with the deity is thus attained, while at the same time ritual actions can be enacted by virtue of the pot's inherent affordances as a vessel. Due to the fluvial nature of this entire streambed, it is unclear whether this vessel actually originated from a context related to the cemetery, nearby shrines, or was indeed intended as a ritual skull replacement, however, the connections to pre-Roman Celtic practices is undeniable.[46]

Another face pot, dated to between the mid-second to later-third-century C.E., was found within a votive shaft at Verulamium and offers a much clearer relationship to the practice of cranial substitution and deposition. Shaft AET measured 3.4 m deep and contained a very striking collection of materials.[47] A human skull, purposefully defleshed either at or shortly after death, was placed with the bones of a young dog at the very bottom of the shaft and then directly covered by a thin layer of clay. Directly above this was then another layer containing the bones of a puppy and fragments of a face pot. Multiple other shafts at Verulamium produced face pot fragments but what is particularly interesting here is that in some instances the pots had been purposefully broken apart to remove their faces, including the pot in shaft AET. The physical destruction of the face here is mirrored in the skull of shaft AET wherein the individual had suffered a fatal head injury and then was purposefully defleshed before deposition.[48] In these instances, both the skull and the face pot are symbolically stripped of the media characteristics that signaled their capacity for Goffmanian agency—that is, their faces—and are reduced to the same status as votive objects. While this example may seem to contradict the points made above about face pots' capacity for agency, it still proves to showcase their capacity to be treated and handled in parallel ways to living and deceased human agents and bodies.

Conclusions

While the aim of this inquiry has not been to present a fully comprehensive approach to face pots as proxies for human agents, it has presented a new realm of possibility in engaging with this unique class of vessels. This has been accomplished by both highlighting lacuna in previous scholarship and engaging the objects in question with frameworks and ideas not yet considered. As a result, based on Iron Age ideologies regarding the human body, and anthropological approaches to bodily engagement, affordances necessary for identity containment, and communicative signaling, we can understand Romano-British face pots as more than simply Roman military materials, but as foreign goods incorporated into local practices and needs. This is an entirely novel approach to these vessels and opens the door for more integrated studies of Romano-British face pots to be seen not only as the products of militarized colonization but also as material tools of local cultural persistence and identity performance in the face of large-scale sociocultural change.

More work is still needed on these vessels and this must first be supported by compiling recent finds and unpublished face pots with definitive proveniences to supplement our current corpus, which overwhelmingly comprises finds with little-to-no contextual data prior to 1950. This is especially true of sherds that, compared to whole funerary vessels, are lacking in both clear contexts and consumption-based approaches. For example, domestic finds of face pots have garnered little attention and more work could be done on how such fragments relate to domestic assemblages as a whole. Kiln face pots, which comprise nearly one-third to a quarter of face pot finds in Britain, could also present a fascinating insight into pottery production and pottery networks of creators and consumers in the Roman period.

Overall, Romano-British face pots are a rich corpus of materials about which we still have much to uncover. This study has shed light on one aspect of these vessels previously overlooked by showing how they acted as proxies and substitutes

for human agents and human bodies in contexts with connotations of and connections to persistent Iron Age practices
in Roman Britain.

Notes

[1] Braithwaite's (2007) seminal catalogue of Roman face pots includes vessels with multiple faces and of distinctly different mor-
phologies from "standard" face pots, including flagons, beakers, and
jars. For the purposes of this study, such vessels will not be included,
and I will instead only engage with the globular, short-necked vessel
forms that are standard among face pots and described above.

[2] See the work of Pitts (2005, 2008) on globalization and glo-
calization models regarding the consumption of Roman material
within provincial contexts.

[3] See Hodder 2004; Hoskins 2006. Cf. Tilley 2001; Gell 2012.

[4] Gibson's (1979) original concept of ecological affordances has
been productively brought into the realm of material studies, most
notably here by Norman (2013) who takes the concept of material
and physical affordances and combines them with ideas of visual signaling (see below).

[5] Knappet et al. 2010.

[6] Warnier 2001, 2006.

[7] Warnier 2006, 187.

[8] Warnier 2001, 4–5, 7, 11.

[9] Warnier 2006, 193. See also Norman (2013, 5, 49–50) on how
object design and style interact with human perception and reaction,
both cognitively and emotionally, in order to convey meaning and
object-purpose through visual signaling.

[10] Knappett et al. 2010. See also Rebay-Salisbury (2010) on ceramic vessels as replacements for bodily containment.

[11] Belting 2011, 9.

[12] See Fowler 2004, 38.

[13] Goffman 1967.

[14] This substitution of ceramic container for human body is
made plain by Tilley (1996, 318) who contends that "a connection
between pots and bodies is clear in the occurrence of face pots, or
pots with eyes.... Smashing a pot with a face is metaphorically like
smashing and destroying a human body, or more specifically another
container."

[15] Webley 2015; Champion 2016. For more in depth study on
preconquest connections to Rome see Creighton 2006.

[16] See Champion (2016) for an overview of work establishing
pre-Roman contacts from Britain to the continent. See also Millett
1990; Webley 2015; Gardner 2016, 490–92.

[17] Hill 2007. Gosden and Hill 2008. Figural art was not entirely
absent from Iron Age Britain, however, it did preference the face
and head over the full human body. See Aldhouse-Green (2004) for
many examples.

[18] Armit 2012. Aldhouse-Green (2004, 189–90) also notes the phenomenon of cranial media across Iron Age Europe, noting that the artistic productions of the time period "was dominated by 'abstraction' and by paucity of mimetic anthropomorphic representation, but the human head, albeit often in distorted form, was a recurrent motif spanning a wide time/space continuum."

[19] See also Cotton 1996. Cf. Ross (1967) on the existence of a cult of the head.

[20] On the Romanization of Britain, see Haverfield 1915; Collingwood and Meyers 1937. On the incompetency of Romano-British art producers to produce classical ideals, see Toynbee 1964; Henig 1995. For postcolonial approaches, see Webster 2001; Pitts 2008.

[21] Romano-Celtic and Romano-Gallic temples, see Forcey 1998. For ritual behaviors, see Fulford 2001. See also Gosden 2005. Aldhouse-Green 2004, 228.

[22] Braithwaite's (1984, 2001, 2007) work remains the only comprehensive treatment of these vessels from across the empire. Her opus magnum (2007) focuses on an extensive catalogue of the face pots, in which she creates a detailed typology of regional categories based on size, facial style, ceramic fabric, and chronology. In her concluding chapters and appendices, she also takes some theoretical approaches to the face pots, concentrating mainly on connections to the Roman military and on tying the pots to other ancient traditions of masks and the worship of Bacchus. For a comprehensive review of Braithwaite (2007), see Darling 2010. Braithwaite (2007) has suggested that cooking could have been within the realm of possibility for these vessels, however, the evidence for burning on the bodies of the vessel or other signs of wear that might indicate such functions is essentially nonexistent. Evidence is complicated by the fact that most pots coming from domestic contexts are fragmentary and those fragments with evidence of the face would have been too far up on the vessel to show signs of burning. Without a fragment containing the facial features or a rim, it is often impossible to discern a face pot from any other local coarse ware. Storage is certainly another potential usage, however, no studies on domestic face pots have been conducted to determine what they once might have contained.

[23] Braithwaite 2007, 351–84. Cf. Aldhouse-Green 2004, 218.

[24] Braithwaite (2007, 352) puts forth that some pots may have been provincial attempts at replicating the more naturalistic mask images from Greek, Etruscan, and central Roman traditions, however, such a conclusion draws on outdated core-periphery models for aesthetic complexity in artistic and material media. Instead, it may prove more productive to consider stylistic divergence from classical models as instances of persistence and even resistance among provincial populations (cf. Aldhouse-Green 2004, 24–27, 215–38).

[25] Jones and Mattingly 2007, 255–352.

[26] Not included in these charts are face pots without definitive provenance and/or provenience. Vessels found at kiln sites have

been included, however, these pots present their own interpretive challenges since they have not been put into conversation with larger kiln studies concerning what populations were being supplied by what kiln sites and when. Future research might consider these kiln-site finds in more detail and how they tied into their local networks of production and distribution.

[27] There is, of course, much also to be said for the fact that the southeast of Britain was more familiar with and had ample contact with Rome prior to the conquest period compared to the rest of the island, however, a fuller investigation of the sociocultural consequences of Late pre-Roman Iron Age contact with Rome lies outside the scope of this study.

[28] Creighton 2006, 14–45.

[29] Aldhouse-Green 2004, 189. Braithwaite (2007, xiii, 10–11, 27–28, 32–37, 457–80 on Roman masks more broadly) has also convincingly shown how continental face pots can be connected to other, related traditions of masks, especially those used for theater, and other facial media intended for apotropaic means. Though the British pots lack the exaggerated features and expressions found on the continental pots, Braithwaite's arguments on the replication of faces and facial imagery are still applicable.

[30] It is worth noting that many potters who accompanied and produced for the Roman army would have been noncombatants themselves and likely would come from the empire's provinces (Fulford 2001). It is very likely that Romano-Gaulish or Romano-German individuals were producing the vessels on the continent and contributed to the iconographic development of the ceramic type as whole, lending them a truly Romano-Celtic nature. See also Cotton 1996, 89.

[31] For funerary contexts with face pots as cinerary urns, it is difficult to ascertain the biological sex or lived gender of the individual interred for two reasons: (1) many cinerary face pots are antiquarian finds and such analyses of the interred individuals has not been undertaken, and (2) face pot burials are not accompanied by objects that might possibly indicate the gender of the deceased. Some decapitation burials utilized pottery with facial features, for example, a decapitation burial at Knobbs Hill farm with a neck-flagon placed above the shoulders (see Collins 2010, 40; see also Crerar [2016, 396] on the deviant nature of this and other related burials), however, there is no current evidence of inhumations utilizing face pots in such a manner.

[32] It is also worth noting that phalluses are a popular motif applied to many continental face pots but there exist no Romano-British face pots with such imagery.

[33] It must be noted that overall, the total number of Romano-British face pots from votive and funerary contexts *combined* (both civilian and military) amount to 44 out of 160 vessels (27.5 percent) with known provenience as per Braithwaite's (2007) catalogue

between 43–325 C.E. If we account for sherds and vessels without definitive provenience, the total number of face pots per Braithwaite (2007) increases to 237 and votive/funerary pots equal 18.57 percent of all pots. Vessels from domestic contexts across all periods account for the majority of vessels (n=116/237, 48.95 percent) while those from kilns account for the second largest percentage of any singular context (n=48/237, 20.25 percent).

[34] On the transformation of the body within cremation practices see Rebay-Salisbury 2010, 64–66. If we consider, too, debates about bodies themselves as artifacts (Meskell 1997; Sofaer 2006) then the transference of agency, identity, and even personhood to funerary objects intended to replicate locales of containment (cf. Knappet et al. 2010) is even more poignant when looking at Romano-British face pots and the levels of social engagement they could potentially have enacted in with other human agents before and during deposition. See also Tilley 1996, 318; Rebay-Salisbury 2010, 68.

[35] Cf. Pearson 1993.

[36] Büster 2021, 976–77.

[37] Huntsman 2014, 143.

[38] Comparable work on objects as human proxies in votive contexts is also relevant here, most notably perhaps I. Winter's (2000) work on Mesopotamian votive figurines as replacements and stand-ins for human worshipers.

[39] Merrifield 1995, 28–31; Cotton 1996, 87–93; Harward et al. 2015.

[40] Cotton 1996, 87–89; Harward et al. 2015, 7–9.

[41] Harward et al. 2015, 105.

[42] Cotton 1996, 88–89.

[43] Cotton 1996, 88.

[44] Braithwaite (2007) has thoroughly demonstrated that face pots are a Roman introduction to England and first appeared only after the initial conquest in 43 C.E.

[45] Cf. Winter 2000. See also Aldhouse-Green 2004, 190–91.

[46] Harward et al. (2015) give a very useful discussion of how natural erosions from the streams in this area have made exact interpretations difficult. While the discovery of the highly concentrated skulls and the face pots would point toward Iron Age practices of decoupling crania from bodies being translated to more palatable formats during the Roman period, the authors are correct to also note that erosion of the cemetery upstream may well have played a larger part in these depositions.

[47] Niblett 1999, 84, 86–87, 254, 256.

[48] Niblett 1999, 415.

Works Cited

Aldhouse-Green, M. 2004. *An Archaeology of Images: Iconography and Cosmology in Iron Age and Roman Europe*. London: Routledge.

Armit, I. 2012. *Headhunting and the Body in Iron Age Europe*. Cambridge: Cambridge University Press.

Belting, H. 2011. *An Anthropology of Images: Picture, Medium, Body*. Translated by T. Dunlap. Princeton: Princeton University Press.

Braithwaite, G. 1984. "Romano-British Face Pots and Head Pots." *Britannia* 15:99–131.

———. 2001. "Masks, Face Pots and Mask Vases." *RCRFActa Supplement* 37:283–93.

———. 2007. *Faces from the Past: A Study of Roman Face Pots from Italy and the Western Provinces of the Roman Empire*. BAR-IS 1651. Oxford: BAR Publishing.

Büster, L. 2021. "'Problematic Stuff': Death, Memory and the Interpretation of Cached Objects." *Antiquity* 95.382:973–85. DOI: 10.15184/aqy.2021.81.

Champion, T. 2016. "Britain before the Romans." In *The Oxford Handbook of Roman Britain*, edited by M. Millett, L. Revell, and A. Moore, 150–78. Oxford: Oxford University Press. DOI: 10.1093/oxfordhb/9780199697731.013.010.

Collingwood, R.G., and J. N. L. Myres. 1937. *Roman Britain and the English Settlements*. 2nd ed. Oxford: Clarendon Press.

Collins, M. 2010. "Knobbs Farm, Somersham: Phase 5B (2) Investigations." Unpublished Report 923, Cambridge Archaeological Unit. DOI: 10.5284/1021186.

Cotton, J. 1996. "A Miniature Chalk Head from the Thames at Battersea and the 'Cult of the Head' in Roman London." In *Interpreting Roman London: Papers in Memory of Hugh Chapman*, edited by J. Bird, M. Hassall, and H. Sheldon, 85–96. Oxbow Monographs 58. Oxford: Oxbow Books.

Creighton, J. 2006. *Britannia: The Creation of a Roman Province*. London: Routledge.

Crerar, B. 2016. "Deviancy in Late Romano-British Burials." In *The Oxford Handbook of Roman Britain*, edited by M. Millett, L. Revell, and A. Moore, 381–405. Oxford: Oxford University Press. DOI: 10.1093/oxfordhb/9780199697731.013.023.

Darling, M. 2010. "Face Pots and the Roman Army – Gillian Braithwaite, *Faces from the Past: A Study of Roman Face Pots from Italy and the Western Provinces of the Roman Empire*." *JRA* 23:643–50. DOI: 10.1017/S1047759400002865.

Forcey, C. 1998. "Whatever Happened to the Heroes? Ancestral Cults and the Enigma of Romano-Celtic Temples." *Theoretical Roman Archaeology Journal* 1997:87–98. DOI: 10.16995/TRAC1997_87_98.

Fowler, C. 2004. *The Archaeology of Personhood: An Anthropological Approach*. Themes in Archaeology. London: Routledge.

Fulford, M. 2001. "Links with the Past: Pervasive 'Ritual' Behaviour in Roman Britain." *Britannia* 32:199–218. DOI: 10.2307/526956.

Gardner, A. 2016. "Changing Materialities." In *The Oxford Handbook of Roman Britain*, edited by M. Millett, L. Revell, and A. Moore, 481–509. Oxford: Oxford University Press. DOI: 10.1093/oxfordhb/9780199697731.013.028.

Gell, A. 2012. "'Things' as Social Agents." In *Museum Objects: Experiencing the Properties of Things*, edited by S.H. Dudley, 336–43. London: Routledge.

Gibson, J.J. 1979. *The Ecological Approach to Visual Perception*. Boston: Houghton Mifflin.

Goffman, E. 1967. *Interaction Ritual: Essays on Face-to-Face Behavior*. Chicago: Aldine Publishing Company.

Gosden, C. 2005. "What Do Objects Want?" *Journal of Archaeological Method and Theory* 12:193–211. DOI: 10.1007/s10816-005-6928-x.

Gosden, C., and J.D. Hill. 2008. "Introduction: Re-integration 'Celtic' Art." In *Rethinking Celtic Art*, edited by D. Garrow, C. Gosden, and J.D. Hill, 1–14. Oxford: Oxbow Books.

Haverfield, F.J. 1915. *The Romanization of Roman Britain*. 3rd ed. Oxford: Oxford Classical Press.

Harward, C., N. Powers, and S. Watson. 2015. *The Upper Walbrook Valley Cemetery of Roman London: Excavations at Finsbury Circus, City of London, 1987–2007*. Museum of London Monograph 69. London: Museum of London Archaeology.

Henig, M. 1995. *The Art of Roman Britain*. Ann Arbor: The University of Michigan Press.

Hill, J.D. 2007. "The Dynamics of Social Change in Later Iron Age Eastern and South-Eastern England 300 BC–AD 43." In *The Later Iron Age in Britain and Beyond*, edited by C. Haselgrove and T. Moore, 16–40. Oxford: Oxbow Books. DOI: 10.2307/j.ctvh1dsh9.4.

Hodder, I. 2004. "The "Social" in Archaeological Theory: An Historical and Contemporary Perspective." In *A Companion to Social Archaeology*, edited by L. Meskell and R. Preucel, 23–42. Malden, MA: Blackwell. DOI: 10.1002/9780470693605.ch1.

Hoskins, J. 2006. "Agency, Biography, and Objects." In *Handbook of Material Culture*, edited by C. Tilley, W. Keane, S. Kuechler, M. Rowlands, and P. Spyer, 74–84. London: Sage Publications. DOI: 10.4135/9781848607972.

Huntsman, T. 2014. "Hellenistic Etruscan Cremation Urns from Chiusi in the Metropolitan Museum of Art." *Metropolitan Museum Journal* 49:141–50.

Jones, B., and D. Mattingly. 2007. *An Atlas of Roman Britain*. Oxford: Oxbow Books.

Knappett, C., L. Malafouris, and P. Tomkins. 2010. "Ceramics (as Containers)." In *The Oxford Handbook of Material Culture Studies*, edited by D. Hicks and M.C. Beaudry, 588–612.

Oxford: Oxford University Press. DOI: 10.1093/oxford-hb/9780199218714.013.0026.

Merrifield, R. 1995. "Roman Metalworking from the Walbrook – Rubbish, Ritual or Redundancy?" *Transactions of the London and Middlesex Archaeological Society* 46:27–44.

Meskell, L. 1997. "The Irresistible Body and the Seduction of Archaeology." In *Changing Bodies, Changing Meanings: Studies on the Human Body in Antiquity*, edited by D. Montserrat, 139–61. London: Taylor & Francis.

Millett, M. 1990. *The Romanization of Britain: An Essay in Archaeological Interpretation*. Cambridge: Cambridge University Press.

Niblett, R. 1999. *The Excavation of a Ceremonial Site at Folly Lane, Verulamium*. Britannia Monograph Series 14. London: Society for the Promotion of Roman Studies.

Norman, D. 2013. *The Design of Everyday Things*. Rev. ed. New York: Basic Books.

Pearson, P.M. 1993. "The Powerful Dead: Archaeological Relationships between the Living and the Dead." *CAJ* 3:203–29. DOI: 10.1017/S0959774300000846.

Pitts, M. 2005. "Regional Identities and the Social Use of Ceramics." In *TRAC 2004: Proceedings of the Fourteenth Annual Theoretical Roman Archaeology Conference, Durham 2004*, edited by J. Bruhn, B. Croxford, and D. Grigoropoulos, 50–64. Oxford: Oxbow Books. DOI: 10.16995/TRAC2004_50_64.

———. 2008. "Globalizing the Local in Roman Britain: An Anthropological Approach to Social Change." *JAnthArch* 27:493–506. DOI: 10.1016/j.jaa.2008.08.003.

Rebay-Salisbury, K. 2010. "Cremations: Fragmented Bodies in the Bronze and Iron Ages." In *Body Parts and Bodies Whole: Changing Relations and Meanings*, edited by K. Rebay, M.L.S. Sørensen, and J. Hughes, 64–71. Oxford: Oxbow Books.

Ross, A. 1967. *Pagan Celtic Britain: Studies in Iconography and Tradition*. London: Routledge & Keagan Paul.

Sofaer, J. 2006. *The Body as Material Culture: A Theoretical Osteoarchaeology*. Topics in Contemporary Archaeology. Cambridge: Cambridge University Press.

Tilley, C. 1996. *An Ethnography of the Neolithic: Early Prehistoric Societies in Southern Scandinavia*. New Studies in Archaeology. Cambridge: Cambridge University Press.

Toynbee, J.M.C. 1964. *Art in Britain under the Romans*. Oxford: Clarendon Press.

Warnier, J.-P. 2001. "A Praxeological Approach to Subjectivation in a Material World." *Journal of Material Studies* 6:5–24. DOI: 10.1177/135918350100600.

———. 2006. "Inside and Outside: Surfaces and Containers." In *Handbook of Material Culture*, edited by C. Tilley, W. Keane,

S. Küchler, M. Rowlands, and P. Spyer, 186–96. London: Sage Publications. DOI: 10.4135/9781848607972.

Webley, L. 2015. "Rethinking Iron Age Connections across the Channel and North Sea." In *Continental Connections: Exploring Cross-Channel Relationships from the Mesolithic to the Iron Age,* edited by H. Anderson-Whymark, D. Garrow, and F. Sturt, 122–44. Oxford: Oxbow Books. DOI: 10.2307/j. ctvh1dj3c.11.

Webster, J. 2001. "Creolizing the Roman Provinces." *AJA* 105, no. 2:209–25. DOI: 10.2307/507271.

Winter, I. 2000. "The Eyes Have It: Votive Statuary, Gilgamesh's Axe and Cathected Viewing in the Ancient Near East." In *Visuality Before and Beyond the Renaissance: Seeing as Others Saw,* edited by R.S. Nelson, 22–44. Cambridge: Cambridge University Press.